"No other generation in human history ha[s] social changes in such a brief time as we [have in recent] years. Whether or not we like these chang[es, they affect the] way we live our lives. In* Sexual Fulfillment, *Herb Chilstrom [and] Lowell Erdahl, retired Lutheran bishops, examine our sexuality in this brave new world with truly open minds and a deep appreciation for our Christian tradition and values."*

—Robert T. Francoeur, Editor of *Sex, Love, and Marriage in the 21st Century* and *The International Encyclopedia of Sexuality*

"For two retired bishops to produce a book on sex is unusual in itself; to do it with the frankness, wisdom, common sense, and grace that pervade this book is not only unusual but makes it a significant gift to the church. In a very readable and concrete style, Chilstrom and Erdahl address issues that rarely receive such forthright and courageous treatment within the church."

—Paul Jersild, Lutheran Theological Southern Seminary, Columbia, South Carolina

"This highly readable book invites all Christian people to enter into realistic (even intergenerational!) conversation about contemporary sexual ethics. The spirit of humility that permeates the entire volume will foster among its readers thoughtful dialogue and careful consideration of issues that many may have found difficult. The authors make strong arguments, sometimes profoundly conservative and other times radically progressive in their conclusions. Few are likely to agree with their every judgment, but most will find their perspective consistent and enriching. Their balanced consideration of tough moral questions is deeply appreciative of biblical wisdom and Christian traditions and enriched by scientific conclusions and the experience of faithful people. As difficult to pigeonhole as it is courageous, this book's moral and pastoral counsel makes a most welcome contribution to our communal task of discerning what makes for sexual fulfillment."

—Patricia Beattie Jung, Loyola University, Chicago

"*This is, from beginning to end, a pastoral book, engaging all of us as both sexual beings and persons of faith. We have a great need to turn down the volume of much of our contemporary discussion, and turn up the level of thoughtful, faithful, sensitive conversation. Chilstrom and Erdahl sit us down in their pastor's study and visit with us out of their faith and experience. They address questions and issues we all live with. They know Scripture, the church, and people very well. Their instincts as pastors shape their writing. This isn't a church policy statement, but rather is the kind of conversation that deepens church life and understanding. It will be widely shared.*"

—Peter Rogness, Bishop, Greater Milwaukee Synod, Evangelical Lutheran Church in America

"*I enthusiastically celebrate this splendid contribution to the sexuality education of the church, even though I would have pushed Bishops Chilstrom and Erdahl further on certain issues. The authors are theologians who know sexuality as intrinsic to God's good news. They are pastors with hearts for real people living with sexual complexity. And they are (praise be!) bishops whose sexual vision and wisdom deserve wide attention throughout the ecumenical church.*"

—James B. Nelson, United Theological Seminary of the Twin Cities, St. Paul, Minnesota; author of *Embodiment*

"*One size does not fit all, but Herb Chilstrom and Lowell Erdahl demonstrate how wisdom from life experience and a willingness to learn from others can result in realistic ethical parameters. They are traditional in tone but open to new information, clear about their priorities but not judgmental about those of others. This gentle guide into contested terrain provides hope that we might all enjoy our sexuality well.*"

—Mary E. Hunt, Ph.D., Codirector of the Women's Alliance for Theology, Ethics, and Ritual (WATER) in Silver Spring, Maryland.

Sexual Fulfillment

for Single and Married,
Straight and Gay,
Young and Old

HERBERT W. CHILSTROM
AND LOWELL O. ERDAHL

Augsburg
MINNEAPOLIS

SEXUAL FULFILLMENT
FOR SINGLE AND MARRIED, STRAIGHT AND GAY, YOUNG AND OLD

Copyright © 2001 Augsburg Fortress. All rights reserved. Except for brief quotations in critical articles or reviews, no part of this book may be reproduced in any manner without prior written permission from the publisher. Write to: Permissions, Augsburg Fortress, Box 1209, Minneapolis, MN 55440.

Scripture passages are from the New Revised Standard Version of the Bible, copyright © 1946, 1952, 1971, 1989 by the Division of Christian Education of the National Council of the Churches of Christ in the USA. Used by permission.

Extract on page 1 from Thomas V. Morris, *Making Sense of It All: Pascal and the Meaning of Life* (Grand Rapids, Mich.: Eerdmans, 1992), 17. Used by permission of the publisher.

"Close to Home" copyright © John McPherson. Reprinted with permission of Universal Press Syndicate. All rights reserved.

"Dear Abby" column by Abigail Van Buren copyright © 2000 Universal Press Syndicate. Reprinted with permission. All rights reserved.

Editorial cartoon by Mike Peters copyright © Tribune Media Services, Inc. All rights reserved. Reprinted with permission.

"Jump Start" copyright © United Feature Syndicate. Reprinted with permission.

"Mother Goose and Grimm" copyright © Tribune Media Services, Inc. All rights reserved. Reprinted with permission.

"One Big Happy" copyright © 2000 Creators Syndicate. All rights reserved. Reprinted by permission of Rick Detorie and Creators Syndicate, Inc.

"Zits" copyright © 2000. Reprinted with special permission of King Features Syndicate.

Cover design by Marti Naughton
Book design by Timothy W. Larson

Library of Congress Cataloging-in-Publication Data

Chilstrom, Herbert W., –
    Sexual fulfillment for single and married, straight and gay, young and old / Herbert W. Chilstrom and Lowell O. Erdahl.
        p.cm.
    Includes bibliographical references.
    ISBN 0-8066-4047-2 (alk. paper)
    1. Sex. 2. Sex instruction—Religious aspects. 3. Sexual ethics. I. Erdahl, Lowell O. II. Title.
HQ31.C5346 2001
306.7—dc21   00-046439

The paper used in this publication meets the minimum requirements of American National Standard for Information Sciences—Permanence of Paper for Printed Library Materials, ANSI Z329.48-1984.

Manufactured in the U.S.A.   AF 9-4047

05   04   03   02   01   1   2   3   4   5   6   7   8   9   10

To Corinne and Carol,
life-giving companions in our ventures of marriage.

≈

CONTENTS

ACKNOWLEDGMENTS

WE ARE GRATEFUL TO MANY PEOPLE who have shared comments of encouragement and criticism during the preparation of this book; many, but not all, of their suggestions have resulted in specific changes in the text. The overwhelming majority of these persons were supportive of our efforts, but we have also been reminded that there are those who will be unable to recommend what we have written. Therefore, do not assume that each one among the following, whose names are listed in alphabetical order, agrees with all of our opinions. Nevertheless, every one of these people has been helpful to our thinking and writing, and we thank them all.

We express our sincere appreciation to: Richard Anderson, Myrwood Bagne, Joan Duke, Thomas Duke, Robert T. Francoeur, Lee Griffin, Stewart Herman, Mark Hollabaugh, Arland Hultgren, Paul Jersild, George Johnson, Vivian Johnson, Randall Lakosky, Susan Leithe, James Nelson, Linda Nelson, William Seabloom, James Siefkes, Daniel Simundson, Brice Smith, William Smith, Elda Soderquist, Ronald Soderquist, Paul Sponheim, Wayne Tellekson, Theodore Vinger, and Harry Walsh.

We also express our personal appreciation to Martha Rosenquist and Henry French of Augsburg Fortress for their encouragement and helpfulness and to Maxine Enfield whose intelligence and word-processing skills produced the five drafts that went into the preparation of this book.

We are also grateful to report that we the coauthors, whose perspectives differ on some subjects, have been able to come to a meeting of minds on the complex and controversial issues of human sexuality discussed in these chapters.

Finally, we thank our wives, Corinne Chilstrom and Carol Erdahl, to whom this book is dedicated, for their life-giving companionship during more than four decades of marriage. Their love and support have sustained us through this writing project as through all of our ventures in life together.

A man once said to me that he had been told all his life there were three topics that should not be talked about in polite company: Religion, Sex, and Politics. Then he went on to add that the older he got, the more he came to realize that these were the only things worth talking about.

— Thomas V. Morris

INTRODUCTION

S EVERAL YEARS AGO, during a coffee-break conversation at a bishops' meeting, we first discussed the possibility of writing a book together on human sexuality. Other commitments kept the project on the back burner until the spring of 1999, when further conversation with each other and encouragement from Henry French, then editorial director for Augsburg Books and Fortress Press, prompted us to get on with it. The result is now in your hands.

This book is for ordinary people. With Dr. French's encouragement, we have aimed for a book that is easy to read, one with a minimum of abstraction and no footnotes. Our goal is a clear and candid sharing of our convictions.

At the foundation of our convictions is the idea of "life-giving sex," a belief that sex is a gift from God as well as a physical reality we live with every day. Only God, of course, can give life. But the beauty of creation is that God invites us into a partnership in which we also are invited to create. When two people bring a baby into the world through the gift of sex, the miracle of creation happens again. When someone by tender affection draws out a loving response from another human being, we help to create a renewed person. Thus while sex in a very narrow definition is what happens when two people have genital sexual activity, it is much more than that. It is a relationship of love and trust that grows over a long period of time and includes the totality of what two people do with each other and to each other.

The word *sex,* of course, is used in many different ways. At times it refers to who we are as sexual beings, as in a birth announcement: "It's a girl!" or "It's a boy!" At other times it refers to what we do, as in the statement: "John and Mary are having sex." Our aim in this book is to set the subject in the broadest possible context while at the same time discussing specific areas of sexual experience. Sex defines who we are from infancy to old age. It's a gift from God, intended to be a blessing for every person for every stage of life. Therefore we understand *life-giving sex* to refer not only to procreation but also to life-fulfilling sexual re-creation.

Sex is about intense and frequent sexual relations early in marriage. But it is also about old love, love that has matured through forty or fifty years and that may involve only occasional intercourse or even no intercourse at all. It is about having children, as well as enjoying intercourse without procreation in mind. It is about the innocent explorations of very young children. It is about how handicapped persons relate to their partners. It is about the attraction persons of the same sex may feel for each other. It is about healthy fantasies.

Most of all, our aim is to help all of us see that sex is about inviting God into this tender, beautiful, sensitive, happy, enjoyable, and spiritual part of our life—our sexuality—and feeling good and comfortable to have God there.

Although this is a joint effort, each of us has taken the lead in writing specific chapters, with the other contributing suggestions and often rewriting parts of chapters. We have undertaken this writing with mixed feelings and even some fear and trembling. Some family members and old friends will not like what we have written. We've been tempted at times to quietly fade away and to let others wrestle with the complex and often controversial issues of human sexuality. But after years of living, listening, learning, pondering, and praying, we feel compelled to speak our hearts and minds on these vital matters. We believe that we are dealing with not only sex but also issues of truth and justice and, above all, the life fulfillment of human beings. Like Paul, we do not claim to have a specific word from the Lord. But we hope that what we share helps in some small way to reveal truth, correct injustice, and enable true love and life fulfillment.

During our work on this project we have been struck by the fact that we are living in one of the most open and free sexual societies in human history. Media and advertising are saturated with sex, and late-night talk-show hosts speak of sex with an explicit frankness that would have shocked previous generations. Never before in American history has there been such explicit public discussion of sexual matters.

Yet most of us remain exceedingly secretive when it comes to our personal sexual lives. We have dear relatives and friends we have known well for more than half a century with whom we have discussed almost every conceivable subject, including human sexuality in general, but with whom we have never shared a single sentence concerning our personal sex lives; nor have they with us. Such reserve is generally appropriate. It is well that everyone doesn't know everything about us. At the same time, it is well that we do not live lives of sexual insulation and isolation. Hidden fears and frustrations, especially when compounded by ignorance and misunderstanding, do not contribute to joyful sexual fulfillment.

To illustrate how our convictions apply to real-life situations, we conclude all of the chapters, except for the first, with a series of questions and answers. Most of these relate to sexual issues that have been raised in pastoral counseling. Those counseling sessions were obviously much longer and less didactic and directive than our Questions & Answers summaries. We have tried to put the counselee's concerns and our responses into a form similar to that of newspaper advice columns such as "Dear Abby," with the hope of making our sharing specific, concrete, and personal.

We also hope that our book will prompt many of you to discuss these issues with a small group in your congregation. To encourage such conversation, we have included an appendix of discussion questions that focus on sexual issues but do not invite sharing of personal sexual practices or problems. Those are most wisely shared under the seal of a confessional, with a pastor or a professional therapist.

We pray that grace will abound for the total life fulfillment of every reader, and that this will include a joyous experience of life-giving sex. If what we have written helps that to happen, we will be grateful.

1 | LIFE-GIVING SEX

WE BELIEVE THAT SEX IS GOD'S GIFT FOR OUR GOOD. But some people don't think sex is good. When confirmation students were asked, "Why do we have a commandment concerning sex?" some answer, "Because sex is bad." When adults were asked, "What did you learn from your parents and your church concerning sex?" some answered, "Sex is dirty" or "Save it for the one you love." There are those who "demonize" sex. They regard it not as good but as evil.

Conversely, there are those who "divinize" sex; in effect, they worship it. For them sex isn't just *a* good gift but is *the* greatest thing in the world, the be-all and end-all of life. Sex is their preoccupation, the center and goal of their lives.

Zits: *By Jerry Scott and Jim Borgman*

Reprinted with special permission of King Features Syndicate.

Those who divinize sex are caricatured by the old story of a newspaper reporter preparing an article about the thoughts of people who were watching the construction of a Manhattan skyscraper. When asked for their thoughts, some told of the bravery and skill of the workers, others of the brilliance of the architect, some of the millions of dollars being invested. One person, however, surprised the reporter by answering, "Sex!" When asked, "What prompts you to think about sex?" he answered, "Nothing special—I always think about sex!" If sex is the most important thing in our lives, it has, in effect, become our "god."

We believe that sex is good but that it is not "god." Near the end of the Bible's first account of creation it says that "God created humankind . . . male and female," and "God saw everything that he had made, and indeed, it was very good" (Gen. 1:27, 31). Our sexuality is one among many of God's "very good" gifts.

How would you rank the importance of sex in your life? We have been in discussions where the question has been asked, "If you had to choose, would you prefer to be blind or deaf?" We have never been in a group that was asked, "Would you rather lose your sight (or hearing) or your sexuality?" How we answer that question is influenced by many factors, including personal desire, age, and life situation. But however we rank our sexuality among God's many good gifts, its loss is nothing to joke about. Those who have experienced loss of sexual desire or ability to function sexually because of illness, medication, or surgery often confess to grief similar to that brought on by the loss of sight, hearing, or a good friend.

As we rejoice in the gifts of sight, hearing, and good friends, we also rejoice in the gift of our sexuality, and again confess to believe that sex is God's gift for our good. Sex is not bad, nor is it like winning for Vince Lombardi—"the only thing!" Sex is a "very good" gift to be received with joy and thanksgiving.

Although many have attempted to spiritualize it, the Song of Solomon in the Bible is really a long poem that celebrates our sexuality. We join in that celebration and invite you to celebrate with us.

WHAT'S IT GOOD FOR?

If sex is God's gift for our good, what's it good for? We answer: Sex is good for life! Sex is life-giving both in terms of procreation and re-creation. Sex is the means God has chosen to give new life. Sex is also one wonderful means, among many, through which God has chosen to give love, joy, and pleasure to our lives. Following are some perceptions people hold regarding the purpose of sex.

For Procreation Only

Some have believed that sex is only for making babies and that it is lustful and sinful to have sexual relations for any other purpose. Except for couples who are seeking to conceive and are having difficulty doing so, those who live according to such thinking will seldom have sexual relations. They would never have intercourse during pregnancy or after menopause, and they would also abstain if they didn't want more children. A couple who learned during their engagement that one or both could not have children would, if committed to the procreation-only perspective, never have sexual relations at all! We do not affirm this view and are not personally acquainted with anyone who holds it. Some in the history of the church have taught it, but we doubt that it was widely practiced.

We also note that this and the following perspectives, which see sex's essential purpose as procreation, exclude gays and lesbians; people who are transgendered, elderly, or celibate; and some disabled people. We will propose a more inclusive perspective that we believe reflects God's loving intention for all of God's children.

For Procreation Plus Love

Others believe that although sex is primarily for baby-making, it is also for the expression of love between husband and wife. The official teaching of the Roman Catholic Church is that since baby-making is an essential purpose of sex, the possibility of conception must be present in every sex act. But since sexual relations are also for the expression of love, the couple can have sexual relations when conception is not possible. With this understanding of what sex is good for, the Roman Catholic Church officially rules out all "artificial" methods of contraception but does approve of the "rhythm method" of birth control, which involves a couple having intercourse only during times in the menstrual cycle when conception is unlikely. Couples are also free to have sexual relations during pregnancy and following menopause.

There has been, and still is, much debate in the Roman Catholic Church concerning this teaching. It is our impression that the use of contraceptive medications and devices (often prescribed to regulate the menstrual cycle or prevent disease rather than for contraception) is widely affirmed and practiced by Roman Catholic couples in the United States.

For Love Plus Procreation

Many reverse the order noted above; they see the expression of love as the primary purpose of sex, and regard baby-making as a wonderful plus. This outlook may seem to undervalue the great gift of procreation, but that need not be so. While we strongly affirm reproductive powers, we also believe that in the lifetime of a healthy marriage, sexual intercourse is almost always for purposes other than procreation.

Even the celibate apostle Paul affirms sexual relations apart from the purpose of procreation, saying: "Do not deprive one another except perhaps by agreement for a set time, to devote yourselves to prayer, and then come together again" (1 Cor. 7:5).

It is also significant that in almost all of the animal kingdom, females are receptive only when conception is possible. If God had intended human sexuality only, or even primarily, for the purpose of procreation, God could have created us to have sex like animals. But God has something better in mind for us. God created us so that we are capable of being sexually aroused and receptive most of the time, a fact that supports the idea that human sexuality is usually for the purpose of expressing love and on only relatively rare occasions for making a baby.

This understanding enables positive affirmation of contraception. Since the possibility of conception need not be present in every sexual encounter, a couple can rightly thank God for contraceptive medications and devices and ask guidance to use them responsibly.

To those who believe contraception is in violation of the Biblical mandate "Be fruitful and multiply, and fill the earth" (Gen. 1:28), we counter with the reminder that this command is one of few within Scripture that has already been abundantly fulfilled! The problem today is no longer underpopulation but overpopulation, and thoughtful family planning, including wise use of contraception, is now a vital part of responsible stewardship of life.

For Pleasure Only

Some regard sex as purely for personal pleasure. We have problems with this perspective and need to make some careful distinctions. We are not against pleasure. In fact, we believe that we may be called to account for all of the proper pleasures we have failed to enjoy! It is obvious, when we consider our sexual organs, that we have God-given capacities for sexual pleasure. The female clitoris, for example, has no known purpose other than to receive pleasure!

But we also need to beware of what the Bible calls "the fleeting pleasures of sin" (Heb. 11:25). We affirm all helpful, healthful pleasure that is life-giving in the long run. We believe that such pleasure is part of the "life in fullness" (John 10:10) that Jesus came to give, but we warn against enjoyment of pleasures that are hurtful to ourselves or to others.

For example, there are great pleasures in eating. The Bible affirms times of feasting, but it also warns against gluttony, which may be pleasurable but is unhealthy and hurtful. If we care for ourselves with proper self-love, we will limit our culinary pleasures to those that are good for us and for which we can truly thank God. As we shall discuss in the next chapter, it is the same with sex. Life-degrading sex, even if it offers the enjoyment of fleeting pleasures, is to be avoided.

For Pleasurable Love

We affirm life-giving sex that sometimes creates new life but far more often adds joy to life through receiving and giving pleasurable love. For us, sex is primarily good not just for the expression of love and not just for the experience of pleasure but for the loving sharing of pleasure and the pleasurable sharing of love, even in those relationships in which conception is neither desired nor possible.

In her book *Body, Sex, and Pleasure: Reconstructing Christian Sexual Ethics,* Roman Catholic professor Christine E. Gudorf devotes a chapter to sexual pleasure as grace and gift. She affirms sexual pleasure as "the first and foundational end of sexual activity" (106). But she also goes on to say that "sexual pleasure can be evil when it is exclusive—when it is derived either through the inflicting/accepting of pain, or through excluding a partner from pleasure either deliberately or accidentally" (106).

In this regard we lament the barbaric practice of so-called female circumcision, which involves the surgical removal of the clitoris and which is still practiced by some people in some parts of the world. In our opinion female circumcision is an evil used to deliberately exclude women from sexual pleasure in an attempt to keep them from sexual involvement with someone other than their husbands.

Life-giving sex lovingly receives and gives pleasure for which we can truly thank God. This sexual pleasure includes, but is much more than, enjoyable genital sensations; it provides life-fulfilling pleasure to the total person—body, mind, emotion, and spirit. We believe, as we will try to express throughout this book, that kind, caring, committed love provides the setting and the safety that enables the free and intimate self-giving that is essential to the experience of profound and pervasive sexual pleasure.

To sum up, we say again: Sex is good for life! It is intended always to be a life-giving means of receiving and giving pleasurable love and also, on relatively rare but exceedingly vital, wonderful special occasions, for the creation of new life. We believe that the God of love we know in Jesus is on the side of life and that life-giving sex is one of God's great gifts for our good.

2 | LIFE-DEGRADING SEX

WHAT DO A KNIFE, A HAMMER, FIRE, AND SEX have in common? Many things perhaps, but we mention only two: (1) They are all good things that help to make life better and are, in that sense, life-giving; and (2) they can all be used in ways that are hurtful and destructive and are, in that sense, life-degrading. The knife that slices vegetables to eat and the hammer that drives nails to build homes can be misused. Controlled fire warms our homes and cooks our food, but when out of control it can burn down a house and kill its inhabitants. So it is also with sex. This good gift from a loving God can be used in ways that are life-degrading instead of life-giving.

Sometimes the misuse of good things is intentional and malicious, but it is often the result of thoughtless and careless living. The knife slips, the hammer smashes the carpenter's thumb, the gas stove turned too high ignites newspapers left too near and the home goes up in flames. Whether owing to malicious intent or thoughtless carelessness, the result can be destruction, suffering, and even death.

And again, so it is also with sex. Although intended to express love and share pleasure, sex can be used in hateful rape and degrading child abuse, both of which cause great pain and suffering. But even in a loving relationship irresponsible sexual activity can disrupt a marriage, transmit disease, cause unwanted pregnancy, and even bring about the agonizing death of a loved one from AIDS.

Whether hurtful actions involve a knife, a hammer, fire, or sex, and whether they are intentionally malicious or the result of carelessness, there is a Biblical word to describe them: *sin. Sin* refers to all of the attitudes and actions that deliberately, or even unintentionally, cause harm and hurt to ourselves and to others.

There are frustrating physical and psychological problems that can decrease and even prevent sexual life fulfillment. *The Diagnostic and Statistical Manual of Mental Disorders,* Fourth Edition (*DSM*-IV), which is available through many libraries, devotes forty-five pages to "sexual and gender disorders." When such difficulties are present we encourage consultation with a medical doctor or certified professional therapist. We may respond to these conditions in sinful ways, but they are not in themselves sinful. In this chapter we focus on sinful sex and will consider questions such as: "When and why is sex sinful?" and "When is it right and when is it wrong?"

EASY QUESTIONS?

Some will say that these are easy questions because all we have to do in order to find the answers is open the Bible and read what it tells us. For those of us who affirm Scripture as the basic norm and guide for our faith and life, that response seems fair enough until we start reading. When we study the Bible carefully, we discover that there is a diversity of scriptural teachings concerning sexuality. We note, for example, that the Old Testament contains dramatic stories of polygamy and concubinage. Concerning King Solomon it reports: "Among his wives were seven hundred princesses and three hundred concubines." It criticizes the king for letting some of those women lead him into the worship of false gods but says nothing judgmental concerning his sexual activity (1 Kings 11:1-13). Scripture prohibits sexual relations during a woman's menstrual period (see Lev. 15:19-24 and 18:19), but has no specific prohibition concerning a man's having multiple sexual partners. There are provisions for a husband to divorce his wife but none for a wife to divorce her husband. Many biblical scholars believe that the commandments that prohibit adultery and the coveting of one's neighbor's wife (see Exod. 20:14, 17 and Deut. 5:18, 21) have more to do with husband's property rights than with specific sexual activity.

Therefore, to get a Christian answer to questions such as "When and why is sex sinful?" and "When is it right and when is it wrong?" we need to do more than read texts from here and there in Scripture that say something about sexuality.

Let's begin by looking at three very familiar texts: The Ten Commandments, David's affair with Bathsheba, and the Prodigal Son. Most of us know the Ten Commandments (Exod. 20), but have you ever asked yourself why they are arranged in that order? Why not put first the commandment about honoring parents? After all, isn't it true that family life is the foundation for all of society? Or why not put first the commandments about coveting our neighbor's wife and property? After all, isn't greed the root of all our trouble in the world? Or—in light of our theme—why not put first the commandment about adultery and the need for fidelity in marriage? If every husband and wife were absolutely faithful, would not most of the world's problems go away?

Good questions. So why do we put this commandment first: "I am the Lord your God. You shall have no other gods before me" (Exod. 20:2-3)? A moment's reflection will make it clear to most of us. This commandment establishes our relationship with God. This commandment lays the foundation for every commandment that follows. When this commandment is broken, all the others will eventually be broken.

The point is this: From the biblical perspective, the heart of sin is a broken relationship.

Let's look at David. Ask most folks what they consider David's greatest sin and they will quickly respond, "He committed adultery with Bathsheba." But that's not what the Bible says. When the prophet Nathan confronts David for having killed a man in order to take his wife, he goes beyond the great sins of adultery and murder to point out an even greater sin: "You have despised the word of the Lord" (2 Sam. 12:9). And when David repents, he confesses, "I have sinned against the Lord" (2 Sam. 12:13). The text makes it clear that it was David's broken relationship with God that was the cause of his sin against Bathsheba and her husband.

In the parable of the Prodigal Son (Luke 15), the problem started long before the younger son left home. The relationship with his father had been broken long before he went off to see the world and spend his inheritance—and his father's gift. That is why he confesses on his return, "I have sinned against heaven and before you" (Luke 15:21).

These texts illustrate a fundamental lesson that applies to every form of degrading sexual behavior. All are rooted in broken relationships.

Another key to grasping the biblical view of sin is to understand that the Old Testament should be interpreted by the New Testament and that all of the Bible must be read in light of God's central revelation in Jesus Christ. When we do that, we remember that Jesus came that we might have life in all its fullness (see John 10:10), and that he not only taught us to love our neighbors as ourselves (Matt. 22:36-40), but also that we are to love one another as he loves us (see John 13:34).

Under the influence of Jesus, the apostle Paul gives us this summary of all of the biblical commandments that relate to how we are to live together.

> Owe no one anything, except to love one another; for the one who loves another has fulfilled the law. The commandments "You shall not commit adultery; You shall not murder; You shall not steal; You shall not covet"; and any other commandment, are summed up in these words: "Love your neighbor as yourself." Love does no wrong to a neighbor; therefore, love is the fulfilling of the law. (Rom. 13:8-10)

Paul makes the same point in his letter to the churches of Galatia:

> For you were called to freedom, brothers and sisters; only do
> not use your freedom as an opportunity for self-indulgence,
> but through love become slaves to one another. For the
> whole law is summed up in a single commandment, "You
> shall love your neighbor as yourself." (Gal. 5:13-14)

In a similar way Paul reminded the Christians in Corinth that "love builds up." And that "'All things are lawful,' but not all things are beneficial. 'All things are lawful,' but not all things build up. Do not seek your own advantage but that of the other" (1 Cor. 8:1 and 10:23-24).

WHAT, THEN, IS SIN?

From texts like these we see that sin is not just a matter of breaking rules in a book. It goes against people, against life, and, therefore, against God, who wills our life in fullness. It is that which does "wrong to a neighbor." Sinful attitudes and actions are not just bad, they are bad for us and bad for others. Sin is life-degrading, life-demeaning, life-denying, and life-destroying. It is sand in the gears of life. It diminishes long-term joy and increases long-term misery for both the sinner and the sinned-against.

In texts like those above, we see that the opposite of sin is Christlike love. Such love, says Paul, does no wrong to a neighbor and, therefore, fulfills any and all commandments related to human relationships. Where sin tears down, Christlike love "builds up." Sin is destructive and deadly; love is constructive and life-giving.

Christlike love is not the kind of greedy possessiveness that often masquerades under the name of love. Nor is it passionate sexual desire, which may be all that is meant when someone says, "I love you." Such passion in a relationship of caring commitment can be compatible with Christlike love, but apart from such a relationship may be nothing more than self-centered, self-seeking lust.

"Love," says Paul, "is patient; love is kind; love is not envious or boastful or arrogant or rude. It does not insist on its own way; it is not irritable or resentful; it does not rejoice in wrongdoing, but rejoices in the truth" (1 Cor. 13:4-6). Sin is the opposite of such love. It is impatient, unkind, envious, boastful, arrogant, rude, irritable, and resentful, and, in sexual as well as other arenas of life, it often insists on having "its own way."

LOVE IS AGAINST
ALL THAT IS AGAINST LIFE

Because it affirms and is creative of life, Christlike love stands in judgment over all that is life-demeaning and life-degrading. Just as Jesus drove the exploitative money changers out of the temple and denounced hurtful hypocrisy and compassionless legalism, we are called to stand, with him, against all that denies and demeans life, including all forms of life-degrading sex.

In the name of Christ we affirm life fulfillment, including sexual fulfillment, for all of God's children. Standing with Christ in affirmation of life, we are at the same time compelled by Christ to stand against all that is antilife, which is what we understand sin to be. We are sinners who fail to live in perfect harmony with our convictions and highest desires, but, lest there be any question about it, we emphatically declare that we are against all sin—heterosexual sin, homosexual sin, and nonsexual sin.

THE IMPORTANCE
OF LONG-TERM PERSPECTIVE

In judging whether sexual conduct is life-giving or life-degrading, it is essential that we take a long-term perspective. Short-term delight sometimes leads to long-term misery. As the proverb says, "There is a way that seems right to a person but its end is the way to death" (Prov. 14:12). At the moment a "night on the town" may seem enjoyable and life-giving. The next morning, however, it may look quite different, especially if one's drunken recklessness has been the cause of a tragic accident. In a similar way, moments of sexual ecstasy that lead to months and years of regret and remorse are more deadly than life-giving. That which gives temporary delight but long-term hurt is sinful. That which leads to long-term life fulfillment for ourselves and for others is not sinful.

At the beginning of this chapter we raised the questions: "When and why is sex sinful? When is it right and when is it wrong?" We believe the biblical answer is: "Sexual attitudes and actions are sinful when they are life-degrading, and right when they are life-fulfilling—not just momentarily but long-term, indeed lifelong."

In determining whether sexual conduct is life-fulfilling or life-degrading, we must evaluate both the interpersonal relationship between those involved and the specific sexual activity in which they are engaged. We believe that genital sexual activity between unmarried persons is generally life-degrading, in the long run, and therefore it is sinful unless it is in a relationship that is the moral and emotional equivalent of marriage. As note on page 94, we understand marriage to have its center in "vows of love, faithfulness, and commitment declared by the couple to each other and witnessed by representatives of the community. . . . 'Equivalent of marriage' couples are mature persons who have less formally but no less sincerely shared such vows of commitment with each other and have witnessed to this fact by telling family and friends that they have entered a relationship they intend to be lifelong." We also believe that, even in the context of such a relationship, sexual acts that are hurtful and life-degrading, such as a husband forcing sex on his wife, are also sinful. Life-giving sex involves both a right relationship and right conduct.

When we apply this standard, we discover that many kinds of sexual activity flunk the test. Promiscuity, prostitution, and sex between adults and children all lack a right relationship of love, commitment, and mutuality. Most teenagers lack the maturity and stability to create such a long-term relationship. Some states have made it a crime for pastors to have sexual contact with parishioners, doctors with patients, teachers with students, and counselors with counselees. Such laws, recognizing the significant power of professionals over the people under their care, regard such sexual involvement as criminal conduct even when it is consensual. While recognizing exceptions, such as when a pastor responsibly dates and eventually marries a parishioner, we concur with these laws and believe that such sexual activity is generally sinful, criminal, and exceedingly unwise.

We believe that homosexual conduct should be judged by the same standards as heterosexual conduct and can therefore affirm same-sex activity only in those relationships that are in fact the moral and emotional equivalent of marriage (a full discussion of same-sex relationships follows in chapter 6).

We also believe that genital sexual contact without intercourse can also be affirmed only within marriage and relationships that are the moral and emotional equivalent of marriage. The self-pleasuring of masturbation, since it does not involve a hurtful relationship and is not in itself harmful, is also generally acceptable. When obsessive it can hinder life fulfillment, but when gratefully received as what one pastor called "God's gift to the celibate," it can be life-affirming and is clearly preferable to involvement in irresponsible, hurtful sexual relationships. There are also times when it can have a positive place in the lives of persons who are in a committed sexual relationship.

A WORD TO OUR CRITICS

We realize that these perspectives will be criticized from both sides. On the one hand, some will strongly object to our affirming life-affirming masturbation and life-fulfilling same-sex relationships and will accuse us of abandoning the Bible. We believe, however, that our opinions are supported by Christ-centered biblical interpretation. We see ourselves as doing what the first Christians did in the name of Christ when they welcomed Gentiles into the Christian fellowship and said, in effect, that we can eat anything for which we can thank God. In the same sense, we accept all forms of life-affirming sexual fulfillment for which we can, and should, rightly thank God. We see ourselves standing with the admonition and affirmation of 1 Tim. 4:1-5. Note how this text rejects legalistic asceticism and encourages grateful receiving of God's good gifts:

> Now the Spirit expressly says that in later times some will renounce the faith by paying attention to deceitful spirits and teachings of demons, through the hypocrisy of liars whose consciences are seared with a hot iron. They forbid marriage and demand abstinence from foods, which God created to be received with thanksgiving by those who believe and know the truth. For everything created by God is good, and nothing is to be rejected, provided it is received with thanksgiving; for it is sanctified by God's word and by prayer.

Christ-centered biblical interpretation saves us from using the Bible, as it has been used throughout the centuries, to support slavery, racism, and patriarchal sexism. It can also save us from denying sexual fulfillment to those who live responsibly with love, commitment, and faithfulness.

On the other hand, we know there are those who will consider our sexual guidelines narrow and restrictive. They see us as old-fashioned conservatives who are out of touch with the free and open sexual ways of the modern world. If that is true, we still stand by our convictions, and remind these critics of the wisdom and warning of Jesus:

> Enter through the narrow gate; for the gate is wide and the road is easy that leads to destruction, and there are many who take it. For the gate is narrow and the road is hard that leads to life, and there are few who find it. (Matt. 7:13-14)

Jesus wasn't talking about sex when he made that statement, but we think it applies here as in the rest of life. The gate of sexual promiscuity is wide and the road of irresponsible sexuality is easy, and there certainly are many who take these routes. But we are still persuaded that these paths ultimately lead to destruction of the joy and meaning of life. The road of responsible sexuality is narrow and not always easy, but it is as wide as the love of God who has given each of us this good gift to be used in ways that lead to joy and thanksgiving.

QUESTIONS & ANSWERS

Q: I recently visited a sauna parlor where I received what they called a "total massage." I didn't have intercourse but it did involve genital "massage." Do you think I was unfaithful to my wife? Did I commit adultery?

A: We think you are obviously troubled and have profound regret. Although we are sorry for what you are going through, we can't comfort you by condoning what you did. We think you were unfaithful to your wife and that you committed adultery. If that judgment seems severe, ask yourself how you would feel if your wife paid someone to give her a "total massage"?

Since you are sufficiently troubled to make your confession to us, we trust that you have also confessed to God and that you now trust God's forgiveness and pray for strength to resist such temptations in the future.

You don't ask if we think you should tell your wife. If you had, we would confess to be less sure concerning that question. We think that honesty is almost always the best policy but also that there are times when love and wisdom compel us to limit our confession to God and to a pastor or counselor and not to lay the heavy burden of our mistake on our spouse. Candid confession and gracious forgiveness are a wonderful blessing, but if the confession helps us but makes life miserable for our partner it may be better to keep it to ourselves. Whatever you decide in that regard, we hope that your being troubled over what you did will teach you to refrain from doing things that you will be ashamed to share.

Q: I have a terrible confession to make. I have just ended an adulterous affair. My wife knows about it and I have asked her to forgive me. And by the grace of God I hope she will be able to do so.

The most terrifying thing about this affair is that I knew it was wrong but I was powerless to stay out of it. It was as if a powerful magnetic force pulled me into it, and I had no will power to resist. My life was out of control.

Because it is so painful to even think about, I am sure that this relationship will never start up again, but I fear being unable to resist a similar temptation. If I were to get involved in another affair I am sure that it would end my marriage to a woman I truly love and that it might cause me to despair of life itself. I need help. Do you know of anything or anyone that can help me?

A: Reading your letter reminds us of the first step of the Alcoholics Anonymous Twelve Steps: "We admitted we were powerless over alcohol—that our lives had become unmanageable." That certainly doesn't sound like a very helpful statement, but it has proven to be the first step toward recovered sobriety and sanity of millions of alcoholics. The Twelve Steps have become the basis of many other recovery groups, including Emotions Anonymous and Sexual Addicts Anonymous. Their steps toward healing begin with the acknowledgment of powerlessness over their emotions and over their sexual desires. All of these Twelve Step programs witness to the fact that victory often comes not through self-centered struggling and trying, but through surrender and trusting in a power greater than ourselves that can restore us to sanity.

We are not suggesting that you are sexually addicted, but we do strongly encourage you to surrender your powerlessness to the power of the grace of God, and to seek professional counsel. Your pastor, doctor, or marriage counselor will be able to make a referral for you. If your therapist recommends a support group, we hope that you will welcome it as a gift, not as a burden or punishment.

It is significant that self-control is among the fruit of the Spirit qualities that the apostle Paul lists in Galatians 5:22. When we open our lives to the empowering Spirit of God we can learn, as Paul did, that when we are weak in ourselves we can be strong in the grace of God (see 2 Cor. 12:9-10).

Q: I am desperate and hope you can help me. I made a terrible mistake and am devastated by the consequences. While out of town on a business trip I had a sexual encounter and contracted a venereal disease. My doctor tells me that it is not fatal but that it is not curable either. Its a chronic condition that when active is highly contagious.

Here then is my terrible dilemma. I can't tell my wife about visiting a prostitute. It would break her heart and be devastating for our marriage. At the same time, I would never risk infecting her with my disease. We have had a beautiful sexual relationship, but now I don't dare have intercourse with my own wife. Now after more than a month of my telling her that I'm too tired or don't feel well she is beginning to think that there is something seriously wrong with me, mentally if not physically. I feel petrified and paralyzed and don't know what to do. I have thought of just running away or even committing suicide. That would put me out of my misery, but I can't do that to my wonderful wife and children.

When I think of how all this is the result of a stupid time of lousy sex with a prostitute, I feel sick and hate myself. I wish there were some way I could die that would leave my family with lots of money and no awareness of what a fool I have been, but I can't think of any way of arranging that. I pray everyday, "Dear God, please help me. I feel like a damn fool. What do you think I should do?"

A: You are in a terrible situation and we really feel your pain. But now you have confessed your sin and asked for God's help. We don't think you are a "damn fool." You did something that turned out to be a terrible mistake—a sin against God and against your wife—but you are honest enough to acknowledge that fact and to seek help.

After pondering and praying over your dilemma, we see only one way out of it. That is to cast yourself on the mercy of God and of your wife by telling her the truth, not only of your sin but also of your love for her and of your desire for forgiveness. Needless to say, that will be exceedingly painful for both of you and we can't guarantee what the result will be. But whatever happens, it seems far preferable to going on as you are or pursuing the tragic options you have contemplated.

After making your confession, we strongly encourage you and your wife to meet with a pastor or marriage counselor to discuss the future of your marriage and with a medical doctor to discuss the future of your sexual relationship. By the grace of God you may be able to make a new beginning in your life together that may even include a new beginning of a safe and life-giving sexual relationship. We can't promise that, but in the grace of God such things are possible.

Q: I am in my early twenties. For the last several years I have been part of a group of friends and acquaintances who have had lots of sex with lots of people. I have heard some of your ideas about sex and think that you are out of touch with our world. You take sex too seriously. It's no big deal!

I've heard that some people used to wonder if they should kiss on the first date. On most of my first dates I make some moves to explore the possibility of having sex before the night is over. To me, sex is just another part of life, like going to dinner or a movie, bowling, or playing tennis. These are fun things that I can do with lots of people. If it's fun and feels good and nobody gets hurt, why not do it?

Don't worry, I never have sex without protection against both pregnancy and sexually transmitted diseases. I don't want to get stuck paying child support or die from AIDS, but since I'm taking precautions I don't think I'm at much risk.

I might want to get married some day and settle down and have a family, but I'm not ready for that yet, and frankly, I'm having lots of fun. To me, your views seem old-fashioned and outdated and I even wonder if you might be a bit jealous of the fun you missed. Is your having missed it part of the reason you are trying to stop others from having it?

A: You read us right! To us, sex is a big deal!

We also think that your sexual fun and games will not lead to lasting joy and gratitude. That's not because we are jealous or because God doesn't like your having fun and is going to strike you down with some terrible affliction. We think you are traveling a road of superficial sexuality that will lead you and your partners into unhappiness and regret, including sexual experiences that are ultimately unfulfilling.

What you have shared reminds us of the proverb that says, "Sometimes there is a way that seems to be right, but in the end it is the way to death" (Prov. 16:25). We believe that in the long run your experience will be more deadly than life-giving and that you will miss the profound joy and satisfaction of a truly human, committed, faithful, and life-giving sexual relationship. A multitude of one-night stands and short-term relationships may be the best a tomcat or stud horse ever experiences, but we don't think that it's the best for either sexual fulfillment or life fulfillment for human beings. By way of analogy we think that such superficial sex is like eating appetizers your whole life. They taste good and temporarily fill you up. But committed sex is like enjoying a whole fabulous, complex, multicourse, many-flavored banquet that is far more satisfying than appetizers could ever be. Creating and enjoying such a lifelong feast with someone you truly love takes time and trust that can't happen overnight.

We think that you are the one who should be envious of those of us who have known the joy of such lifelong relationships, and we encourage you to get off the road you are traveling before it ends in misery and regret. Please don't take that as a spiteful threat, but as a compassionate warning. We wish you joy but don't think you will find it at the end of the road you are traveling. Therefore we encourage you to get on a new road of in-depth relationship, faithfulness, and commitment, which we believe has far greater promise of life fulfillment, including a truly life-giving sexual relationship.

3 | SEXUAL FULFILLMENT IN MARRIAGE

W E BEGIN THIS CHAPTER with strong and thankful affirmation of marriage. Both of us and our wives thank God for the joyful privilege of being married for more than forty years.

We make this affirmation and confess our gratitude in full awareness of the problems and frustrations that come with marriage. One of us coauthored a book, called *Be Good to Each Other: An Open Letter on Marriage* that begins with a section titled "We Wish You Joy" and follows with a section titled "We Promise You Trouble." It quotes a line from a friend who said that it is both wonderful and terrible to be married—wonderful in its depth of love and understanding and terrible in its potential for misunderstanding and conflict. We agree and are thankful to report that in our experience the wonderful has far exceeded the terrible. At its best, marriage, like love, is a many-splendored thing. In this chapter we will focus on some of the sexual aspects that bring joy to our married lives.

We know that joyful marriage is not everyone's experience. Among our saddest experiences as pastors have been conversations with persons for whom marriage has become a burden instead of a blessing. The latest statistics suggest that about 45 percent of first marriages and 55 percent of second marriages will end in divorce, and that many of those who stay married confess to being unhappy in their life together.

TIMES HAVE CHANGED

Marriage at the beginning of the twenty-first century is very different from what it was one hundred years ago. In those days the primary motive was sometimes practical economics. Marriage provided a means of financial and social security as well as the only respectable setting for sexual activity. Today the motivations are more emotional. When asked, "Why are you getting married?" most answer, "Because we love each other and want to spend our lives together."

Although most couples still have some form of "till death do us part" in their wedding practices, some prefer saying, "As long as love shall last," and, when using the traditional phrase, confess to understand it to refer to "emotional" or "relational" death rather than only physical death. We agree that there are times when divorce enables freedom from slavery to life-destructive marriage. But we also see a lack of commitment and of a willingness to work for renewal that contributes to many divorces.

A person from a culture in which most marriages were arranged by parents rather than based on feelings of personal attraction and love said that our marriages were like putting a hot kettle on a cold stove and that theirs were like putting a cold kettle on a hot stove. He then asked, "Which kettle do you think will stay hot the longest?" We are not advocates of parents selecting spouses for their children. But the fact that some arranged marriages turn out better than some inspired by personal feelings witnesses to the fact that fulfilling marriage needs to be based on something more than physical attraction and emotion.

THE "PLEASURE BOND"

Years ago sex therapists William H. Masters and Virginia Johnson wrote a book called *The Pleasure Bond*. Some of its readers must have been surprised to discover that these liberated authors, who seemed to be free from the "hang-ups" of traditional sexual morality, identified the "pleasure bond" as "commitment" and stated that it is promiscuity that is ultimately boring.

The commitment at the heart of lasting and fulfilling marriage is like the courageous attitude of an adventurer who sets out on a journey of exploration, joyfully determined to see it through. Marriage is more than just a legal document. It is more than a ceremony. Marriage is a couple's personal and public declaration that they intend to live in lifelong faithfulness. Living in that commitment, said Masters and Johnson, provides the safety and freedom creative of the pleasure bond and enables joyful sexual fulfillment. Secure in their shared love, couples are liberated to give themselves to each other and to receive each other with the abandonment characteristic of an adventure of exploration and discovery.

THE ART OF LOVING PLEASURING

Learning to lovingly pleasure and be pleasured by one another, like all great arts, takes time, patience, and much practice. No one can pick up a violin and become a virtuoso in a week. Basics of sexual relations no doubt come more naturally than playing the violin, but the duet of loving pleasuring is no less complex and requires no less skill and practice.

We are well aware of the many jokes, such as that in this comic strip, that poke fun at sex in marriage, but we believe that such jesters are either jealous or terribly misinformed.

Mother Goose and Grimm: *By Mike Peters*

Copyright © Tribune Media Services, Inc. All rights reserved. Reprinted with permission.

This comic might be accurate for couples who have nothing going for them but physical intimacy and sexual attraction, but it is certainly not true for those whose closest intimacy is not just physical, but emotional, mental, and spiritual. They share their hearts and heads as well as their bodies. They discover early in their relationship that the sexiest part of a person is not between the legs but between the ears, and that profound sexual fulfillment involves the sharing of our total selves and not just our sex organs. In such marriages, the wedding cake is truly a foretaste of many feasts to come, and an enhancement of both the sex drive and the promise of years of adventurous sexual fulfillment.

Be Good to Each Other tells of a father who told his son on his wedding day that during their first year of marriage he should put a bean in a jar every time he and his bride had sexual relations and that when that year was over he should remove a bean from the jar after each sexual encounter. The father then declared, "The jar will never be empty!" We feel sorry for a father who could make such a statement. He and his wife never learned the art of sexual loving. We hope that son and his wife, in spite of his father's terrible counsel, learned in their experience the joy of long-term, life-giving sexual relations that would only slightly diminish in frequency while being enhanced in quality year after year in their life together.

Although some cynics liken marriage to slavery or a prison, we think that marriage is more like a garden—a place of warmth and tender nurturing in which beautiful flowers bloom and nutritious food grows. George Bernard Shaw is reported to have said, "Marriage is popular because it combines the maximum of temptation with the maximum of opportunity." That may be true, but we think that it provides more than temptation and opportunity. It provides the loving inspiration and the loving receptivity that makes life-giving sex a lasting adventure. If that seems like an exaggerated expectation, we have to confess that we have no experience beyond our forty plus years of marriage. But we are encouraged by reports that healthy couples have fulfilling sexual relationships into their seventies and eighties. We continue to look forward to this dimension of our lives together and will have more to say about it in chapter 7, "Sexual Fulfillment in Elder Years."

SEX AND GRACE

Before we turn to some of the specifics that can produce sexual frustration and sexual happiness, we should say a word about grace and sexual fulfillment. From our Christian perspective, all of life, including all of marriage and all of sex, is lived in the context of grace, which is (a) the loving presence of God that surrounds and welcomes us every moment, (b) the loving power of God that continually sustains and strengthens us, and (c) the forgiving mercy of God who assures us that we can start over again when we have failed. With the apostle Paul we believe that "nothing can separate us from the love of God," and with the author of the first letter of John, we believe that "we love because God first loved us" (see Rom. 8:38, 39 and 1 John 4:19). Grace enables us not only to give ourselves in joyful surrender and openness to the love of God but also to give ourselves lovingly to others, including in a very special and exclusive way to our partner in marriage. Sexual fulfillment occurs when grace enables us to live with loving abandon—freely, mutually, tenderly, and fully giving and receiving the pleasurable love we have for each other.

Those of us who are Lutherans have had it dinned into us from our childhood that we do not save ourselves by our good works, yet we continually need to relearn the fact that salvation comes by trusting and not by trying. This is also true in terms of our sexual relationship. No one, for example, can become sexually aroused by will power alone. A man can't will an erection; nor can a woman will an orgasm. We can only be open to the thoughts and stimuli that create arousal and response.

We can't achieve sexual fulfillment by trying harder. But we can receive it, and we can give it! Here again the teaching of Jesus comes true in experience. When we, in greedy self-centeredness, hold back from gracious giving and receiving, we miss the meaning and joy of life. But when we lose ourselves in the adventurous abandonment of loving and being loved, we experience a meaning and joy that is possible in no other way.

Therefore, while we acknowledge that it is often necessary to work at all aspects of our marriage, including communication, financial planning, and our sexual relationship, we also believe that the atmosphere surrounding times of love should be more like a playground than a tense workshop. In that setting of warmth and grace, we can lovingly and playfully give ourselves to one another, focusing more on the pleasure we can provide than on the pleasure we can take, and remembering all the while that openness to receive the pleasuring of the other is also a vital form of giving.

SEXUAL FRUSTRATION IN MARRIAGE

In this context we will now attempt to address more specifically the question of why some marital relationships are sexually fulfilling and others are sexually frustrating. We don't think the reason is that couples don't desire and hope for joyful fulfillment in every area of their married life. Our conversations with couples in premarital counseling confirm the results of the recent Rutgers University study that indicates that almost all couples enter marriage with high expectations. In some cases they may be so unrealistically high that they virtually guarantee disappointment.

Observant couples learn early in their marriages that there are rhythms in life together. Sometimes we feel so tender and affectionate toward one another that we wonder how we could ever have an unkind thought or feeling about such a wonderful person. But then something happens that makes us so angry we wonder how we could ever care for such a person at all! We also learn that there are rhythms in our sexual experience. Our sexual relations, as *Be Good to Each Other* points out, are sometimes like a seven-course candlelight dinner and sometimes more like stopping by McDonald's for a hamburger. We wish every couple many "fancy restaurant" experiences but encourage them to expect some "stops at McDonald's," which can also be life-giving.

Specific Sexual Problems

Granting these rhythms and variations in sexual experience, we go on to ask, "Why are some sexual relationships so frustrating and unfulfilling?" Recognizing the complexity of an adequate answer to that question, we begin our response with the reminder that people who love each other and who live by the grace of God still have lots of personal problems.

From our counseling experience and the testimony of therapists, we know, for example, that some men are able to maintain sexual relations for only a few seconds, which may be long enough to create a pregnancy but leaves the husband frustrated and the wife unfulfilled. Sometimes a solution is as simple as a loving husband's learning to abandon his wham-bam-thank-you-ma'am approach to intercourse. Men need to constantly remind themselves that it often takes a woman much longer to become ready for full and enjoyable intercourse. Sometimes a half hour or more of loveplay (we like that word better than *foreplay* and will say more about it in the Questions & Answers section at the end of the chapter)—tender stroking and gentle stimulation—will not only prepare her for intercourse, but will also enhance pleasure for the man. There may be situations, of course, when the help of a sex therapist is needed. Most couples will find, however, that kind and candid conversation and openness to learn from one another will unlock the door to greater and greater sexual fulfillment.

While spontaneous "stops at McDonald's," referred to earlier, may be appropriate at times, studies indicate that intercourse itself, especially when brief, does not provide fulfilling stimulation for most women. Therefore, since they may not be in the mood to do so afterward, husbands need to learn how to pleasure their wives prior to intercourse and their wives need put aside their modesty and guide them to gently and patiently do so. Having been gifted with a clitoris, women need to learn and to teach how its purpose can be lovingly fulfilled. When lack of female response is a problem, couples are encouraged to remember that "orgasmic capacity in females increases with age" and that "many females increase their orgasmic capacity as they experience a wider variety of stimulation and acquire more knowledge about their own bodies" (*DSM*-IV, 505). There are, however, exceptions, and some older couples, as we will discuss in more detail in chapter 7, need to give special time and attention to learning how to best satisfy each other. We also note that the Food and Drug Administration has approved a device to be sold only by prescription, to help women experience orgasm. Readers with this concern are encouraged to consult with their doctors.

We don't think that the apostle Paul was thinking of sex when he wrote "Love is patient; love is kind" and love "does not insist on its own way" (1 Cor. 13:4-5) but we believe that it applies here, as to every dimension of life. Even when there are frustrating sexual problems, couples can usually learn to be good to each other in ways that are more, rather than less, satisfying. When this is not possible and problems create ongoing difficulties in a relationship, the couple should attend a workshop or retreat on marriage or seek the help of a competent therapist.

Relationship Problems

In our learning from therapists and our experience as counselors, we have come to believe that the majority of sexual problems in marriage do not arise from specific dysfunctions or disorders but rather from stresses and strains in the relationship between husband and wife. It is difficult to have a satisfying, let alone truly life-giving, sexual relationship when one is filled with resentment, disgust, or fear of one's partner. Although it is true that having sexual relations can sometimes help to heal a troubled relationship, a more common situation is that troubles in the relationship undermine sexual fulfillment. It has often been said that what happens at bedtime is affected by how a husband and wife treat each other at breakfast. That's not to suggest some breakfast-time techniques for getting more or better sex, but it is a helpful reminder that our sexual experiences are part of the total tapestry of life.

In situations where specific sexual problems are disturbing the marital relationship, the chief need is to solve the sexual problems, with the help of a sex therapist if necessary. But when the sexual problems are the result of difficulties in the marriage relationship itself, the chief need is to solve the marital problems, with the help of a marriage counselor if necessary. Our attitudes and actions have consequences. There is an old saying that "when we pick an apple we shake the tree." Almost everything we say or do can either shake or steady our marriages.

CONSIDER THE CONSEQUENCES

Even when we intend no harm we often say and do things that turn out to be hurtful. By way of illustration, we recall the story of a man who intended to go to Detroit, and boarded a bus. Unfortunately he paid no attention to where the bus was going and after a long day's journey discovered he was in Kansas City. His experience provides a vivid reminder of the fact that the destinations to which we come in life are determined not by our intentions alone but by the roads we travel, and that we had best be attentive to signs along the way. Although intending to arrive at lifelong marital happiness, we may live in ways that bring us to discord and divorce. Although sincerely desiring joyful, life-giving sex, one or both may behave in ways that lead to sexual frustration and discontent.

In these painful experiences we also discover that while it takes two to make a marriage work, it takes only one to end it.

Some of our saddest counseling experiences relate to situations where one partner is eager to work at making the marriage better but the other says, "I've had it!" refuses to seek help, and calls it quits. When there are signs that a marriage is traveling in the wrong direction, couples need to honestly share their frustrations long before they've "had it." They need to help each other or seek outside help before it is too late.

Remembering that our deeds sometimes have negative consequences that we did not intend can help us to live in ways that lead to gratitude instead of grief. When wrestling with difficult decisions, Abraham Lincoln was in the habit of asking himself, "How will I feel about this decision five or ten years from now?" When tempted toward a fleeting pleasure, we would do well to ask ourselves that question. If we think we will regret it, we should be wise enough not to do it! Millions of smokers dying from the results of their addiction have wished that they had acted in accordance with that wisdom. So did one man whose marriage was ruined by an adulterous affair. He spoke for many when he didn't just say, "How could I be so sinful?" but "How could I be so stupid?" Living under the grace of God does not mean living without consequences. Wise decision making involves careful consideration of consequences, and courageous choosing that opts for long-term joy—not only for ourselves but for those we love—instead of the fleeting fun of self-indulgence.

What We Bring to Marriage

We grieve with those who have learned these harsh realities in relation to their own or their partner's premarital sexual promiscuity. We have been struck by the fact that many spouses who were promiscuous themselves are resentful of their partner's premarital experiences, fearful of unfavorable comparisons, and doubtful of their partner's present and future faithfulness. Such conversations undergird our conviction that one of the great gifts a couple can bring to marriage is their premarital faithfulness to each other.

One agonizing question that we have encountered is: "Should I tell my fiancé about my sexual experiences, or should I lie about them?" Our bias is in favor of the truth. A foundation of lies is a shaky basis for marriage. At the same time, we recall comments made in regard to both pre- and extramarital relationships, by spouses who said, "I wish he (or she) had never told me. It only made matters worse." It has been said that every virtue needs to be balanced by other virtues. We are to be truthful, but we are also to be kind. When courageous people lied to save Jews from the death camps, the virtue of compassion overruled the virtue of truth telling. But such situations are exceedingly rare. We are persuaded that the pain and disruption of honesty is almost always preferable to the corrosive effects of deception and dishonesty. If we don't know what to say, we might be well-advised to consult with a professional counselor or spiritual adviser before saying anything.

Wrestling with this issue is another reminder of the fact we are generally wise to refrain from doing things that we need to keep secret. If we don't want our present or future wife or husband to know about it, it is best to refrain from doing it.

At the same time, we are aware that we can't undo the past and that forgiveness is essential to any long-term relationship. Without condoning sexual sins, Jesus seems to have been even more severe in his judgment of the sanctimoniously self-righteous who refused to forgive. He reminds us that we are all sinners and that grace abounds to welcome each of us with all of our faults and failures. We are told to "be kind to one another, tender-hearted, forgiving one another as God in Christ has forgiven you" (Eph. 4:32) and that we are to "welcome one another" as God in Christ has welcomed us (Rom. 15:7).

It's difficult to forgive, and painful to confess and be forgiven. Both are often beyond our personal capacity, but neither is beyond the healing, life-transforming power of the Spirit of God. In openness to that Spirit, we can pray not only our confessions of sin, but also our confessions of inability to forgive, and trust that in honest openness to God we will be enabled to be honest, open, and welcoming of one another.

Beyond whatever our personal premarital indiscretions may have been, we also bring to marriage all of the positive and negative sex-related understanding, misunderstanding, and experience we have known. This may include sexual abuse, incest, rape, and a host of rigid, legalistic attitudes that we may have "caught" as well as been taught by our parents, pastors, and other significant adults. We also bring our personal physical and emotional histories, which, in addition to all of their strengths, may include experiences with illness, stress, anxiety, depression, and medications that may affect our sexual desires and abilities. We think it is almost always wise for couples to tell their life stories to each other and to share their deepest hopes and fears. Such is the stuff of which real intimacy is made.

QUALITIES OF A
LIFE-GIVING SEXUAL RELATIONSHIP

Having considered some of the problems that can hinder sexual fulfillment, we now share reflections on some of the qualities of a life-giving, life-long sexual relationship.

Mutual Love

We begin by emphasizing the importance of mutual love and caring for one another. At its best, being in love with someone involves much more than being sexually attracted to that person. Sexual attraction is only part of marital love. True love wills and works for the joy of the one we love. It seeks, as we have emphasized earlier, not just to get but to give. When such love is mutual, there is more joy to receive and to share than is possible in any other way.

For example, imagine two couples. One couple focuses on taking as much as possible of everything, including attention, time, money, and sexual satisfaction from each other. The other couple focuses on giving as much as possible of everything, including attention, time, money, and sexual satisfaction to each other. Which couple do you think will experience the most satisfaction in their marriage and in their sexual relationship? One can almost guarantee that the first couple will be miserable and the other joyful. We say "almost" because we know that tragic illness, accident, or other like circumstances can strike the most loving and giving relationship. Therefore, we don't promise perpetual happiness to anyone, single or married. But we still believe that those who live by the love of God and who share graciously in their relationships with others find far more joy and fulfillment in every aspect of life than those who greedily seek to take all they can and to give as little as they can.

Mutual Respect

Related to mutual love is mutual respect that witnesses to the essential equality of the relationship and to the absence of coercion and manipulation. We believe that it is difficult, if not impossible, to have an intimate relationship with someone who is regarded to be superior or inferior to us. As we noted earlier, it is a crime in some states for those in positions of power to take sexual advantage of those under their influence—adults with children, pastors with parishioners, doctors with patients, employers with employees, etc. This doesn't mean that a pastor and parishioner or doctor and patient should never marry, or that high-powered people can never have life-giving marriages and sexual relationships. But it does mean that if they do not have a sense of personal equality in spite of their differences, and are lacking in mutual respect, the chances of marital and sexual fulfillment are significantly diminished.

Couples with a basic sense of equality and sincere mutual respect are also fortified against the temptation to use coercion, manipulation, or bribery to get their way in their marital and sexual relationships. A marriage license does not give a husband the right to rape his wife, nor should a wedding be the beginning of a relationship of matrimonial prostitution in which a wife provides "tricks" for her husband in exchange for financial favors. These are extreme situations, but there are a lot of subtle, and not so subtle, varieties of such coercive, manipulative behavior.

We grieve for mothers whose sexual experience has been so deadly that the best they can teach their daughters is to do their duty to their husbands by submitting to their sexual demands however burdensome the experience may be. We hope that daughters who have been indoctrinated with such grim expectations will be pleasantly surprised to discover through the tender affection of their loving husbands, that they can both, as one wedding service puts it, "find delight in each other" and that they will thereafter think of their sexual relationship in terms of mutual delight rather than wifely duty. In that setting wives will feel free to delight their husbands by initiating sexual overtures and won't be the passive responders in every sexual encounter.

Mutual Openness

In addition to mutual love and mutual respect a third characteristic of a lifelong, life-giving sexual relationship is mutual openness to learn from and to teach one another. We hope that every couple discovers early in their life together that there are specific sexual behaviors that they both find pleasurable and satisfying.

At the same time, we alert couples to expect that there are some things that are a "turn-on" for one but a "turn-off" for the other. Such differences often cause marital conflict that takes time and loving patience to resolve. We have, for example, counseled with couples who were in serious conflict concerning oral sex, and it hasn't always been the husband who expressed such desires. It is sometimes the wife who finds such stimulation satisfying.

In response to concerns such as these, we first confess that we do not agree with those who regard all sexual activity, except for intercourse in the so-called missionary position of man over woman, to be sinful and perverse. We believe that couples are free in the grace of God to be creative in their lovemaking. That does not mean, however, that they are free to harm or humiliate one another. With that reservation we concur with the old pastor who was reported to have told a young couple who were bold enough to inquire about such things, "When the door is closed, anything goes."

In counseling in such situations we also recall the old saying, "In matters of taste there is no disputing." If one person likes spinach and the other can't stand it, there really isn't anything to argue about. The same is true sexually speaking. If one is thrilled by a certain sexual practice but the other finds it figuratively, or literally, distasteful there is not much sense in continually bickering and fighting about it.

That doesn't mean however that the couple is sexually incompatible or that one or both must suffer lifelong marital frustration. In response to specific points of difference we believe that couples should focus on enhancing all of the other areas of their sexual relationship that they both find satisfying instead of trying to pressure a reluctant one to do what he or she is uncomfortable doing. In such situations the pressuring person does well to remember another old saying: "We don't make the beans grow by pulling on them!" When the pressure is off and the mood is right, the reluctant one may even discover the loving courage to surprise the spouse by trying some new things that had previously seemed out of bounds.

Some of us who still can't stand cooked spinach have discovered, to our surprise, that spinach salad is delightful, and that foods we were sure we wouldn't like turned out to be tasty. The strange character in Dr. Seuss's famous story was certain that he did not like green eggs and ham but after turning them down on many occasions finally decided to try them and was amazed to discover that "I do so like green eggs and ham! Thank you! Thank you, Sam-I-Am." In a tender, loving relationship we may be emboldened to try some new things and may be pleasantly surprised at what we discover.

In his devotional classic *My Utmost for His Highest*, Oswald Chambers speaks of the Christian life as an adventure of abandonment. "In our abandonment," he says, "we give ourselves to God just as God gives himself to us, without any calculation," and "when you get through to abandonment to God, you will be the most surprised and delighted creature on earth; God has you absolutely and has given you your life." As we give ourselves in trusting abandonment to the love of God and receive new life each day as a gift of God's love, so also we give ourselves in the abandonment of loving sexual surrender to one another and share in the life-giving renewal of this good gift from God.

Mutual Faithfulness

Having affirmed mutual love, respect, and openness to learn from and to teach each other, we conclude this section on the qualities of a lifelong, life-giving sexual relationship with emphasis on the importance of mutual faithfulness. Since we have underscored the importance of mutual respect and equality in our marriages, you will not be surprised to note that we also affirm the freedom, and indeed the responsibility, of both husbands and wives to fully utilize their God-given abilities. At its best, marriage affirms the partners in their individuality as well as in their union and enhances rather than stifles their creativity. From our perspective this means that both partners have lots of freedom to pursue their individual interests and live out their personal vocations. But at the same time, we strongly affirm the importance of sexual faithfulness to one another. Adultery not only goes against the biblical commandment; it goes against our spouse, against our marriage, against our family, and even, in a significant sense, against all of our trusting relationships. In the broadest sense, adultery tears away at the fabric that holds society together.

Although husbands and wives rightly share many aspects of their lives with others, we believe that their genital sexuality is a personal gift to be shared with no one else. Some churches regard marriage as a sacrament. Even those who do not give it sacramental value believe that in the grace of God marital sexual relations can be described as sacred. They are personal means of grace conveying love for one another reflective of the love of God that enlivens and embraces both partners.

We also underscore the fact that there are many kinds of unfaithfulness in addition to those that are specifically sexual. Spouses who deceive, betray, or withdraw from their partners may be just as unfaithful as those who have illicit sexual relations. The faithfulness we affirm is emotional, mental, and spiritual as well as physical.

We believe that the biblical calls to total faithfulness are not arbitrarily imposed from above. They are not true just because they are in the Bible; they are in the Bible because they are true! They witness to the realities of life and are revelations of the fact that we are created to live with trustworthy commitment and faithfulness. The laws of love, as E. Stanley Jones liked to say, are written not only in the text of Scripture but into the very texture of life.

An extremely troubled young man once came for counseling. He told about how he and his girlfriend, with whom he was having sexual relations, had agreed at his insistence that theirs would be an open relationship and that each of them was free to have sexual relations with others. He now believed that she might be exercising that freedom and was amazed to discover that he was terribly upset by the thought of it. "I don't know what's the matter with me," he said. "I was the one who insisted on such freedom. I think I must be in love with that girl!" He was learning in the painful school of his own experience that there is something very special about sexual relations and that true love, in contrast with exploitive lust, requires commitment and faithfulness. His experience reminds us of what we quoted earlier from Masters and Johnson—the pleasure bond is commitment, and "promiscuity is ultimately boring."

There are those who will respond with a "Yes, but . . ." They will point out that there are lots of relationships that fall between "true love" and "exploitive lust," and will ask, "What about situations where there is mutual sexual attraction between persons who are caring friends? They may never get married but they will not do anything that would deliberately hurt or exploit each other."

CONCERNING EXTRAMARITAL RELATIONSHIPS

Please ponder this statement: Our trust is created by the people in whom we have it! That is, trust is built over a long period of time as each person learns the other can be relied upon. It witnesses to one of the most basic realities in all human relationships including marriage. If we trust our spouses, it is because their trustworthiness has evoked and sustained our trust. If someone says, "I am going to try to trust my spouse today," there is something wrong in the marriage.

One thing wrong with extramarital affairs is that they undermine and often destroy the trust that is essential for a life-giving relationship. The discovery of such an affair is often devastating to a marriage. By the grace of God and the sharing of forgiveness it is sometimes possible to maintain and even strengthen the marriage, but not without much pain and suffering. Even if the affair can be kept secret, it still has a corrosive effect on the marriage relationship. The lies and deception necessary to keep it secret are difficult for the deceiver to live with, and they often create suspicions, which are countered by more deception, creating an ongoing cycle of dishonesty and growing distrust.

We wish that people tempted to indulge in extramarital sex could hear some of the confessions of regret that we have heard in our counseling ministries. Many of these do not lament their sin-fulness but their stupidity. Most don't say, "How could I be so wicked?" but "How could I be such a fool?" often with an expletive for emphasis. We have read the testimony of Christians who claim to be living honestly and happily in sexually open marriages, but we are not persuaded that it is possible to have relationships that are the "moral and emotional equivalent of marriage" with multi-ple partners and, therefore, we cannot affirm such forms of polygamy. We don't think that such relationships hold much promise of being life-giving in the long term, and that they are far more likely to result in pain and regret for everyone involved.

There are also those who tell of being thankful for affairs that led them out of miserable marriages into a new and joyful rela-tionship. That may sometimes be true, but we have lived long enough to observe that relationships that began in deception and dishonesty often disintegrate into another separation or divorce. This observation may be born out by the Rutgers "State of Our Unions" study, which points out that "second and subsequent marriages have a higher divorce rate" than first marriages.

A woman shared during a counseling session that she discov-ered orgasm in an extramarital affair. That discovery, in turn, greatly improved her sexual relationship with her husband. Nevertheless, that affair was one of the significant factors that eventually destroyed the marriage. In retrospect we believe it would have been far better for that wife to have made that great discovery with her husband, who could have learned, even via the kind of gentle suggestions we have made in this book, to make sexual relations more pleasurable for his wife.

When there are problems in marriage, including the sexual relationship, we believe that marriage counseling, conversations with a sex therapist, or even reading a good book on marriage and sexual fulfillment offer more promise of marital healing and life-giving sex than does an extramarital affair. In times of trouble we should seek help and healing, not attempt to escape into the dream world of a new relationship. If it becomes necessary to end a marriage, both parties should beware of too quickly entering into rebound relationships; they too often turn out to fit the old adage about going from the frying pan into the fire. There are those who, as another old saying puts it, "marry in haste and repent in leisure" and probably even more who remarry (or get wrongly involved) in haste and repent in sorrow. Granted, it is possible for an extramarital affair to lead to an equivalent of marriage relationship and eventually to marriage itself. Still, we believe it is generally far wiser for tempted persons to find renewal in their marriages or, if that is impossible, to end the marriage before becoming sexually involved with someone else.

We know that living is a complicated business and that there are subtle and significant differences in human relationships, but we are not persuaded that sexual attraction in a caring friendship is a safe and secure basis for sexual relations. It is our conviction that mutual faithfulness, together with mutual love, mutual respect, and mutual openness to give and receive in the abandonment of loving are the solid foundation upon which the house of a truly committed, lifelong, life-giving sexual relationship is built. We believe that mutual love, mutual respect, mutual openness, and mutual faithfulness add up to the mutual commitment that is essential for marital sexual fulfillment.

QUESTIONS & ANSWERS

Q: When we visited with the clergy person who will conduct our wedding, we learned that we will be required to go through an extensive preparation for marriage program. We agreed to do it, but we don't like it. We are both college graduates and think we know how to get along with each other without that kind of instruction. Do you think this requirement is fair?

A: We are glad you are willing and sorry that you are resentful. In our experience most couples find such programs to be enjoyable as well as helpful. They recognize that marriage is a great and often difficult adventure and are eager to learn everything they can to make it for better instead of for worse.

We wish that couples would spend as much time and energy, to say nothing of money, preparing for their marriage as they spend on their wedding. Being poorly prepared for the wedding may cause some embarrassment. Being poorly prepared for marriage is a tragedy. Therefore, we encourage you to consider the pre-marriage program as an opportunity and not just an obligation, and to give yourselves to learn everything you can from it. We wish we had had such an educational experience before we got married and are grateful for programs like Prepare and Engaged Encounter that are now available almost everywhere. In marriage, as in so much of life, we need all the help we can get and are sure that if you are receptive to what the program offers, you will find it helpful. If your pastor weren't offering it, we would encourage you to seek it elsewhere.

Q: My husband is a cross-country truck driver who is away from home more than half the time. We visit via phone almost every day and some of those conversations get pretty sexy, and are frankly satisfying for both of us. Need I say more? Do you think this is sinful?

A: You need not say more. One of us was asked the same question in a counseling relationship years ago, and it may be more common than any of us may realize.

It goes without saying that there is nothing in the Bible about telephone sex, but there is a lot about love and faithfulness.

We believe that sexual morality has more to do with the relationship between two people than with their specific sexual activity, unless it is in itself harmful. Since your telephone sex occurs in a relationship of marital love and commitment, we don't believe that it is sinful. Apart from such a relationship, we believe that it would be sinful. In your case, we believe that it gives you another reason to thank God for each other—and for Alexander Graham Bell.

Q: We love each other and have a wonderful sexual relationship, but we are having a terrible time finding time to be alone together. One of us is a night owl and the other is a morning person. It seldom seems that we are in the mood at the same time. We also have young children and are fearful of one of them barging into the bedroom in an embarrassing moment. All of this has caused a lot of bickering between us. What do you advise?

A: First of all, we encourage you to stop your bickering and to focus together on solving these problems. We are often amazed and pleased to see the good things that happen when couples stop blaming each other and direct their attention to correcting the things that trouble them.

We think that the first thing that you should do is to get a lock for the bedroom door and to teach your children that your bedroom is "Mommy and Daddy's private place."

Jump Start: *By Robb Armstrong*

Reprinted by permission of United Feature Syndicate, Inc.

Finding time to be alone together is a common problem in early-bird/night-owl marriages, but with persistence and planning it can usually be solved. There are usually some times when you are both wide awake. How about making a date for love shortly after the kids are sound asleep? So what if the dishes are still in the sink and the house isn't picked up? The night owl can do that later, or the early bird can do it in the morning. That's only one option among many. Plan ahead and surprise one another with your creativity.

We also encourage you to live out what someone has called "the multiple honeymoon plan." Plan for some regular times away from your children. These need not be expensive. Perhaps you and another couple can arrange some time each month when you take care of each other's children so both couples can have some time alone. Or maybe the children can stay with grandma and grandpa or some other friends or relatives while you have time alone at home. That's not always easy, but it's often possible. Love and creativity go well together. We encourage you to be both loving and creative in all aspects of your marriage.

Q: We have seen ads in the daily newspaper for sexually explicit videos that are described as being "educational and an enhancement to sexual fulfillment in marriage." Would it be sinful for a Christian couple to watch and perhaps learn from such videos?

A: We have seen such ads but have not seen the videos. But we must confess that most of the little we have seen of pornography strikes us as being antiwoman and even antisex. Pornography presents a false model of human sexuality. It treats women as playthings and sex as a superficial, self-satisfying recreational activity.

At the same time, we don't believe that everything explicit is necessarily pornographic. A joint seminary/medical school educational experience, designed to help pastors and doctors counsel and treat parishioners and patients, made use of several sexually explicit films. A few were commercial pornography that soon became boring, but many were portrayals of caring love. This educational experience enabled pastors and doctors to be more comfortable and candid in dealing with sexual issues raised by their counselees and patients. Perhaps the videos you are tempted to watch can also be helpful to some marriages.

If you decide to watch them, it may be wise that you do so together so that you can then discuss not only what you have learned, but also what you have experienced emotionally. You may discover that your reactions are similar or that they are exceedingly different. It seems to be generally true that men are more stimulated by sexually explicit materials than are women. Test that stereotype by sharing your honest reactions with one another. Student evaluations of that seminary/medical school sex education program indicated that the small-group discussions following the films, rather than the films themselves, were the highlight of the program. We expect that your couple conversation following the videos will also be the most important part of your educational experience. If that proves true, you may feel grateful instead of guilty for watching them. We also believe that there are good books that serve the same purpose. A visit to a bookstore and a look at books related to human behavior and human sexuality will give you a good cross-section of this material.

Q: When I look at our wedding pictures and then see myself in the mirror I wonder how my husband can still be attracted to me. I have gained a lot of weight and no longer have the figure I had then. He says he still loves me and even jokes kindly about my love handles. I am frankly embarrassed over how unsexy I must appear to him and am reluctant to initiate lovemaking for fear of being rejected.

A: We have a twofold response. First of all, we remind you the sexiest part of a person is the brain, not the body. Physical attractiveness can certainly be a great sexual enhancement, but it's not central. We have sometimes been surprised in our counseling experience to work with couples who are physically attractive but who have miserable sex lives and, on the other hand, to deal with other couples who have self-images similar to your own but have an active, life-giving sexual relationship. We suggest that you tell your husband how you feel about yourself and about him. And then, when the mood is right, be bold in initiating lovemaking. Both you and your husband may be pleasantly surprised at what happens.

Our second response is to suggest that if you really are overweight and out of shape and are as troubled by it as you seem to be, that you quit berating yourself and instead take action to lose weight and get in shape. Visualize the person you would like to be and surrender yourself to a structured regimen of diet and exercise that will enable you to become that person. Don't try to do it on your own. As long as you are trying, you are still depending on yourself. As in so much of life, the secret is often not in the struggle but in surrender. Not surrender to the problem, but to the good Lord and the good people who can empower you day by day to decrease your consumption and increase your physical activity.

Q: I have just read *Be Good to Each Other*. I want to tell you, it has prompted me to get a divorce! If what's in that book is marriage, my husband and I haven't had a marriage for over twenty years! We have been to a counselor, and I have tried everything I can think of, but nothing seems to work. I don't think I can go on like this. Would it be wrong for me to get a separation or divorce?

A: We were surprised to learn that reading *Be Good to Each Other* prompts you to seek separation or divorce, but your explanation makes your reaction understandable. We believe that couples should do everything they possibly can to preserve and strengthen their marriages, but we also know that when a marriage has really died the most respectable thing may be to have a funeral for it. We are not advocates of separation and divorce. But neither do we believe there is any virtue in maintaining marriages that are destructive for someone, and often everyone, involved. Taking marriage vows is exceedingly serious, but there are times to acknowledge, as did Abraham Lincoln, that "promises [one] should never have made in the first place are better off broken than kept."

Jesus said some strong things concerning divorce and remarriage that should also be taken seriously (see Mark 10:1-12 and Matt. 19:1-12). We should remember, however, that these statements stand in the context of the mercy and grace Jesus so clearly reveals. When his disciples protested the severity of some of these sayings, Jesus replied, "Not everyone can receive this teaching, but only those to whom it is given. . . . Let anyone accept this who can"

(Matt. 19:11-12). These words lift those sayings out of legalism and into love, and, we believe, open the possibility of responsible divorce and remarriage. The God we know in Jesus is on the side of life, and we believe, as we have tried to indicate throughout this book, that God stands against all life-denying, life-degrading, life-destroying relationships and in favor of all that gives true meaning and joy to life.

Nevertheless, we are unsure concerning your specific situation. Have you really tried everything? Are you open to more in-depth counseling? Are you open to attending a Marriage Encounter weekend? Many have found this not only helpful in making good marriages better but sometimes in making bad marriages good. Are you open to participation in the Retrouvaille program? *Retrouvaille* is a French word that means "rediscovery." It is similar to Marriage Encounter, but focuses on the rediscovery of hope and meaning in troubled marriages. Marie Pate, its international executive coordinator, says, "Marriage Encounter saved our marriage, but Retrouvaille healed our marriage." You can always get a divorce, but we don't think you should do so until every possibility for healing has been exhausted.

In spite of the pain and absence of true marriage for the last twenty years, you still need to ask yourself, "Do I really want a divorce? Will our children and I really be better off without him than with him?" If the answer to those questions is no, we encourage you to do more to save and to heal your marriage. If the answer is yes, we give you our blessing. Whatever you decide, we assure you that God's all-sufficient grace will be with you to guide and sustain you through all your ventures of living.

Q: My spouse and I are frequently frustrated over differences in our desire for sex. We love each other and don't want to either coerce or reject one another. How do you suggest we deal with these differences?

A: First of all, we commend you for sharing your frustration with one another. Too many couples sulk instead of talk and that never makes things better. We also affirm your discomfort with both being pressured and being rejected. Those are painful experiences and you are wise to recognize that your differences in sexual desires are stressful to both and not just one of you. Remembering that fact gives you common ground on which to stand together and can help keep you from self-righteously criticizing and blaming each other.

There is an old saying that "it is futile to argue with feelings." If one of you feels amorous and the other doesn't, it doesn't do any good to argue about it. There are, however, some helpful things you can do.

Close to Home: *By Mike McPherson*

Helen tries out her new "Not-Tonight-Honey" nightgown.

CLOSE TO HOME *copyright © John McPherson. Reprinted with permission of Universal Press Syndicate. All rights reserved.*

To us the key of living with such differences is to bring together mutual respect and mutual openness. Mutual respect means that if one of you is totally unable or unwilling to have sexual relations, there will be no coercive attempt to pressure you into doing so. Mutual openness means that amorous overtures will not be rudely and rigidly rejected. In a mature and healthy marriage we lovingly do a lot of things for each other even when we don't feel like doing so. Such loving favors aren't always very romantic and may involve trips to the bank, post office, or grocery store, or even vacuuming the rug and washing the dishes. It may also involve times when we lovingly give of ourselves and have sex with our partner even when we don't especially feel like it. Yet we are often gratified by the experience. If such "giving in" leaves us angry and resentful instead of thankful, it would have been better to have made a date for future lovemaking instead of doing it under duress.

Following these suggestions won't eliminate all of your frustrations. They come with the territory and are part of life whether we are single or married. Our most important suggestion may be to encourage you again to care for each other, and to seek in every possible way to give your partner the gift of joy. When you both do that, you will still have many differences but they won't create as much frustration and conflict.

Q: I have a problem you may never have heard of before. I am a happily married man and I love my wife. I don't think there are any specific problems in our sexual relationship, but I have to confess that I prefer masturbation to intercourse. I have been married five years and we have sex together once a week or so and I often engage in self-pleasuring between those times that I find more satisfying and never dare tell her about. Is there something terribly wrong with me? If so, what can I do about it?

A: Your experience is not unheard of. We have counseled with others in the same situation and also with women who find self-pleasuring more satisfying and orgasmic than intercourse. Nevertheless, we think that you and your wife may well have a problem that needs to be faced and dealt with. In self-pleasuring you are in control of your fantasies and don't need to relate to another person. Intercourse finds its beauty and fulfillment in the depth of the interpersonal relationship. Therefore, we think that this is a situation that calls for kind and loving sharing with one another. To deepen your relationship you need to kindly tell each other what you find pleasurable and thereby learn from and teach each other. When you learn to lovingly give pleasure to each other we believe that it will prove to be more fulfilling than sex in solitude.

From our chronologically advantaged perspective, it appears that you haven't been married very long and are both beginners with much to learn. We encourage you to be kind to each other in every aspect of your life together and wish you many joyful times in your ventures of loving and learning.

Q: I am a public school teacher and must confess to having developed a special fondness for one of my colleagues with whom I work very closely. I look forward to our times together and feel like I did when I was a teenager and had a crush on somebody. I have had fantasies about having sexual relations with him! We are not teenagers. We are both married and have children. I have been extremely discreet and don't think that he has any idea of how I feel about him, nor has he given any indication that he has similar feelings toward me. We have talked about lots of things and I have been tempted to drop some hints concerning my feelings or even to bluntly tell him the truth. I have also wondered if I should tell my husband. I feel that I am being dishonest and deceptive. What do you think I should do?

A: We think that you have done the right thing by telling us and by not telling either your friend or your husband. What good would that do? Wouldn't telling make things more difficult both at school and at home?

The New Testament says that we are to speak "the truth in love" (Eph. 4:15). That means that we are not only to be honest and truthful, but also that we are to be loving and kind. We think, for example, that it would be exceedingly unloving and unkind for a husband to make a point of honestly telling his wife about every woman he meets whom he finds more attractive or for her to tell him about every man she considers more handsome.

For you to tell your teacher friend of your feelings strikes us as a seductive move that will either be rejected to your embarrassment and the disruption of your friendship or be accepted with greater danger and potential misery for both of you. Such feelings, we believe, are wisely shared only with a trusted confidant such as a pastor or counselor and not with the person involved nor usually with one's spouse. On many issues husbands and wives can have therapeutic conversation with each other, but usually not in regard to the kind of concerns you raise. These are best shared with a wise and compassionate outsider.

Q: We have a good marriage, but there is one thing that bothers my husband and is increasingly frustrating for me. He wishes that I were more affectionate and would like me to cuddle up with him when we are watching TV together. I would like that, too, but have discovered that whenever we get cuddly and affectionate, he interprets it as a sign that I am eager for sex. He then feels hurt and rejected when he discovers that's not what I had in mind. I think we have a good sexual relationship but wonder why we can't be loving and affectionate without getting sexually involved. Is there something wrong with me? Or with him? Or with both of us?

A: We don't think there is anything wrong with either of you. Your concerns are among the most common complaints we have heard from both wives and husbands.

You don't tell us how long you have been married or how well you communicate verbally. It sounds as if your husband needs some help in understanding your body language. He seems to think that all affection is a seductive invitation and you seem to have responded nonverbally by withholding affection. We encourage both of you to kindly verbalize your feelings. The deepest intimacy of marriage is not just physical sex but emotional sharing. If you respectfully share what is in your hearts and minds we believe that you will learn that it is possible to have times of affection without specific sexual involvement that will be gratifying for both of you.

Q: During the 30 years of our marriage I have been perplexed by something. To be blunt about it, I'm a horny guy and think a lot about sex. I have the impression that my wife hardly ever thinks about sex, and if I didn't initiate it I doubt that we'd often have sexual relations.

But at the same time I also discover that when I do take the initiative, which is quite often, she is not only receptive but is exceedingly responsive. In fact, I think she is often far more responsive than I am!

Don't get me wrong. I am not complaining, but I am puzzled and wonder if we are normal or a bit perverse?

A: We don't think you are perverse at all. In fact, to be as frank with you as you have been with us, we congratulate you on your great sexual relationship.

Although there are exceptions to every stereotype and great dangers in generalizing, it seems to be true that most men are more specifically preoccupied with sex than most women (some, as this comic suggests, may prefer TV).

Mother Goose and Grimm: *By Mike Peters*

Copyright © Tribune Media Services, Inc. All rights reserved. Reprinted with special permission.

At the same time, it may also be true that most women have greater sexual capacity than most men. Masters and Johnson are bold to assert that "there is no question that the human female is infinitely more effective as a sexual entity than the male ever dreamed of being. Her potential capacity to respond to effective sexual stimulation is almost unlimited." Since women are able to have multiple orgasms, this is certainly true physiologically. At any rate, we trust you will be more grateful than envious over your wife's responsiveness, and that both of you will continue to find joy and fulfillment in this dimension of your life together.

More specifically, does your wife know how you feel about her failure to take initiative in sexual relations? Are you so assertive that she never gets a chance to do so? Confess your feelings to each other and kindly respond to what you learn.

Q: I am soon to have a hysterectomy. My doctor assures me that my situation is not life-threatening, but both my husband and I are worried that this will ruin the beautiful sexual relationship we have enjoyed for many years. Do you think this is something we should be worried about?

A: If your experience is typical you need not be concerned. The May 2000 Mayo Clinic Newsletter reports that "There's encouraging news for women who fear a hysterectomy is the end of an enjoyable sex life—the opposite may be true for some" and that "A hysterectomy may improve sexual function for some women." A hysterectomy removes nothing essential for your continued sexual fulfillment. For some women elimination of the possibility of pregnancy brings greater sexual freedom and pleasure.

There are those, however, whose experience is not typical and who do experience a lack of sexual desire and response. If your ovaries are removed, you will need to have a frank discussion with your doctor concerning replacement of the female hormones estrogen and progesterone. If you are troubled by diminished sexual desire, ask your doctor about the possibility of adding a small amount of testosterone to your hormone medication. It seems to influence sexual desire in both men and women, but because of possible side effects needs to be carefully evaluated and monitored. Therefore, be sure to have frank conversation with your physician or with a specialist in hormone treatment. We also encourage you to lovingly teach your husband to be patient in lovemaking and to share the time and tenderness necessary for your mutual fulfillment.

Q: I think that sensuous touching is the best part of sex. My husband thinks that foreplay is a waste of time and that we should skip that and get to the real thing. This is causing conflict between us. Do you think that there is something wrong with me? Or with him? What can we do to resolve this conflict?

A: We don't like to take sides in marital conflict, but this time we side with you. One of the problems with the word *foreplay* is that it gives the impression of being like the appetizer before the main course. It is often that way, but need not be so. We prefer the word *loveplay,* which can sometimes be a very satisfying full-course dinner!

We also note survey reports indicating that many women, like yourself, experience sensual touching as the best part of sex, and that when they are open to receive as well as to give such touching, most men find it pleasurable enhancement to their sexual fulfillment.

In their book *Let Me Count the Ways: Discovering Great Sex without Intercourse,* Marty Klein and Riki Robbins point out that "outercourse, which involves a variety of erotic and often playful sexual activity, can be as fully satisfying as intercourse and for some people even more gratifying."

We encourage you to share these thoughts with your husband and hope that he will receive them not as criticism, but as an invitation to join you in an adventure of more intimate and sensuous loving.

Q: We read somewhere that the sexual goal of marriage is for the husband and wife to experience simultaneous orgasm. We have been married for more than ten years and by that standard are sexual failures. What can we do to solve our problem and reach that goal?

A: From our perspective, your only problem is in having the wrong goal. We agree with Ruth S. Jacobowitz, author of *150 Most-Asked Questions About Midlife Sex, Love and Intimacy,* that "it is one of the great myths of all time that mutual simultaneous orgasm is the objective of good sex. It happens rarely" (137). A more realistic and far better goal is a mutually satisfying, life-giving sexual experience.

Q: We have an active and somewhat satisfying sex life, but something seems to be missing. Even though we have been married for several years, there are times when I feel like we are still strangers. What can we do to get closer to one another and to also have a more fully satisfying sexual relationship?

A: We have often said that the closest intimacy in marriage is not the physical intimacy of sharing our bodies but the mental and emotional intimacy of sharing what is deepest in our hearts and minds. We doubt that it is possible to have the most fully satisfying physical intimacy without similar depth of mental, emotional, and even spiritual intimacy.

For that to happen, we need to be both vulnerable and trusting in our life together. We need to let down our defenses, tell of our hopes, fears, and dreams, and let our partners know who we really are.

That is scary business, and it is difficult and maybe even impossible, if we don't have a kind and caring partner who helps us feel safe and secure enough to be open and honest with one another. Letting down the barriers to mental and emotional intimacy is a prelude to letting go physically and emotionally in our sexual relationship.

"Letting go" is a big theme in both religion and recovery programs. The motto "Let go and let God" is often heard in Christian preaching, and often seen on the walls of Alcoholics Anonymous and other Twelve Step meeting rooms. In letting go to God, we cease self-centered struggle and striving and rest our lives in the love and power of God. In letting go to each other in marriage, we open our hearts and minds to share and to receive our deepest thoughts and feelings and also to give ourselves with loving abandon to love and be loved in the sharing of emotional and physical sexual intimacy.

To enable this to happen, we need to tell each other with both kind and honest words and tender and loving touching what turns us on and then to do all we can to lovingly fulfill our partner's emotional and physical sexual desires. When we both do that, we discover in our own experience that loving sexually, as in every other way, is truly life-giving.

4 | SEXUAL FULFILLMENT WHEN SINGLE

WE NEED TO SAY AT THE OUTSET that this chapter and the next chapter were by far the most difficult for us to write. Like our readers, we're in touch with the world. We know from studies, from surveys, and from many personal conversations that sexual intercourse is common among those who are single. For that reason, we have written and rewritten these chapters, searching for a way to address this reality while holding to what we believe to be a worthy and attainable ideal—that sexual intercourse is best reserved for the nurturing context of relationships of marital commitment.

ALL OF US ARE INCLUDED

We know, of course, that each of us spends part of life as a single person. We all start out that way. Some are single between marriages. Because of death and divorce, more than half of those who marry live again as single persons. And for some, all of life is lived as a single person. We live in a society where marriage and family are stressed so heavily that it may come as a shock to learn that, according to the U.S. Census Bureau, nearly 45 percent of adults in the U.S. are single.

Because we are inclined to link sex with genital activity, it's easy to associate it only with marriage or with the relationship between two persons who choose to have a genital relationship apart from marriage. In fact, however, sexuality is a part of our very being. Though subtle and associated largely with the unconscious, we begin to have sexual feelings when we are very young children. Sometimes without even realizing what is going on a youngster may act out early sexual feelings. This is quite normal.

As we begin moving into our teen years, our sexual feelings become more specific. Most of us are drawn to people of the other sex. Some experience sexual attraction to persons of the same sex. Others have sexual feelings for both their own and the other sex. This chapter will be devoted to some thoughts about the majority who develop strong and usually exclusive feelings for persons of the other gender. Most get married. Some, though they have such feelings, do not get married.

SINGLE PERSONS
HAVE SEXUAL FEELINGS

It's a great mistake to assume that intense sexual desire can be set aside until marriage, that someone who does not marry has no interest in sex, or that formerly married persons lose desire for sexual intimacy. For a great variety of reasons, some people simply do not marry or remarry. There's nothing abnormal about being single.

That needs to be said in a culture in which it's assumed that one should marry and in which single persons are so often the target of biting comments about their sexuality. They are hounded at times with cruel questions: "When are you going to find Mr. Wonderful?" "Isn't it about time you made some woman happy?" Even parents are often guilty of dropping not-so-subtle hints about wanting to be grandparents. Single persons usually brush off the words as though they don't hurt. But in their heart of hearts they often feel the sting and long for a world where they can be free from such unkind treatment.

LOOK IN THE RIGHT PLACES

For those who desire marriage and a sexual partner, we strongly urge that you begin by looking in the right places. There are many options open to single persons: music ensembles, museums, support groups, garden and photography clubs, dance lessons, tour groups, political parties, community education courses—the list could go on and on. We are told that one of the best meeting places these days is the browsing and coffeehouse sections of high-class bookstores where people can strike up conversations that begin with books and move on to personal acquaintance. The important thing is to choose an area that is of genuine interest to you. If you meet someone who becomes your mate, well and good. If not, you have enriched your life in a pursuit where you already have a strong interest.

You won't be surprised, then, that we also suggest church as a good place to find a partner. Many churches, especially larger congregations, have active singles groups where happily married couples have met their match. But we're also all too well aware of the fact that most churches ignore singles and have little or nothing to offer them. Singles tell us that they often feel like a "fifth wheel" in some congregations. One way to deal with this is to find other singles and take the initiative yourself in getting a group started in your church.

And why not try the Internet? We all may have once thought that this was an odd way to meet a prospective mate. But computer matching services have been online for many years and have proved to be effective in many cases, some known to us. Aid Association for Lutherans, for example, has a Web site for those looking for a mate with Christian values. You can visit the site at *www.aal.org* and then click on "Lutherans Online" followed by "Single? Mingle!" Again, however, we urge caution. Fantasy can overpower reality when we meet someone on the Internet. Be very cautious and recognize that this is only the first in many steps of getting to know a person who could be a potential partner in marriage.

In all of your enthusiasm for finding a partner, there is one cardinal rule that every single person should honor: Married persons are off-limits. If someone already married shows an interest in you, it is your responsibility to set boundaries. You need to give that person a clear message that you're not in the game of breaking up marriages and families.

WHY NOT ENJOY BEING SINGLE?

But what if nothing works? What if Ms. or Mr. Wonderful never shows up? Is it possible one can enjoy being single and unattached? We think so. We both have good friends who surely would have preferred to be married. But when it became apparent that this was not to be, they didn't shrivel up and die! On the contrary, they found wholesome outlets. Some have formed deep, nonsexual friendships with persons of the same gender. They enjoy traveling together, going to church, seeing movies, and all the things good friends can share. Some have found satisfaction serving others by working in soup kitchens, visiting the sick and elderly, and engaging in community service and many other activities.

Single persons sometimes forget some of the positive aspects of being unattached. You may have more money to spend than if you were married—and surely more discretion with how to spend it. You have personal freedom to order your life as you wish. Take a trip on the spur of the moment. Enjoy the privacy, quiet, and comfort of your home. Plunge into the adventure each day brings. Unlike one who is married, you never know what a casual contact with someone you have never known before may bring. After many years as a single person and after significant career achievements, a friend of ours met a widowed classmate at a high school reunion. Within a few months they were married. Now she looks back on a very full and enjoyable life as a single person while she enjoys the new venture of a later-than-usual marriage. It may not happen for you, but it could.

DESIRES THAT WILL NOT GO AWAY

Even when you have come to the place in life where you are reconciled to being single, what should you do with those desires that won't go away? As we have said earlier, there are many who have very strong feelings of attraction for a person of the other sex, but never marry. Others are single between marriages or after a marriage and sometimes for long periods of time. How should these persons deal with sexual feelings in an appropriate way?

Our advice and counsel will be controversial in some circles. But it's based on the assumption that we are created by God as sexual beings and that the worst thing we can do is to pretend that this is not so. Repressed sexual feelings and desires will almost certainly come out in inappropriate ways.

We think there is a better way—self-pleasuring. The Bible never refers to masturbation. Like anything else in life, it can, of course, be destructive if one makes it an end in itself. But sex is a normal human appetite. Like hunger, it can be satisfied in appropriate ways. As with eating, moderation and good sense should be one's guide. You need not feel guilt about it. If God has given you sexual desire, is it not reasonable to believe that God also gives ways to satisfy that desire?

Self-pleasuring often involves an imagined sexual relationship with another person. For that reason, a word needs to be said about that comment of Jesus in the Sermon on the Mount about looking lustfully at a woman. We remember that Jesus said, "Whoever looks at a woman lustfully has already committed adultery with her in his heart" (Matt. 5:28).

What did Jesus mean? That sexual desire is wrong? That it is inappropriate to have a sexual longing for another person? We surely don't think so. There may be help for us in an unexpected source—the Apocrypha. This volume is a collection of fourteen books that were included in the Bible up to the time of the Reformation and are still regarded as Holy Scripture by Roman Catholics and some other Christians. Among these books is one entitled "Susanna." It's the story of "A very beautiful woman . . . who feared the Lord" (Sus. 2). She became the object of the lustful preoccupation of two respected elders who were determined to have intercourse with her. The text reads: "They conceived a passion for her . . . their thoughts were perverted . . . they were smitten with her . . . they desired to have relations with her . . . they watched jealously every day for a sight of her" (Sus. 9-12).

It is interesting to note that the Greek word used to describe their passion for Susanna is the same word used in the Sermon on the Mount when Jesus says, "Whoever looks lustfully." It's likely that Jesus knew the story of Susanna. If this is what Jesus had in mind when he spoke of lust, one can safely say that it's not the same as fantasy thoughts that have no intention of being acted out.

We also think it's wise to put these words of Jesus into the context of marriage. Our Lord's concern was for the sanctity of marriage. He condemns the one who—as one of the commandments suggests—covets his neighbor's wife. Jesus does not have in mind a natural impulse to have an appropriate sexual relationship. Rather, his concern is with lust that is predatory, that is out to get what one wants no matter what it may cost another person. We have heard the testimony of women who tell us that sometimes they can feel themselves being "visually undressed" by some men who leer at them with obvious intent. An appreciation for a beautiful woman—or a handsome man—is one thing, a good thing. Lustful looks and repeated episodes of imagined predatory sex are quite another.

We believe that the ability to imagine and fantasize is a gift from God and that our lives would be poorer without it. We also believe that just as there are life-giving and life-degrading sexual actions, there are also life-giving and life-degrading sexual fantasies. For an engaged couple, for example, who are deeply in love to vividly imagine what it will be like to have sexual relations with each other would, we believe, be both a normal and healthy fantasy. For someone to be obsessed with fantasies involving adultery (which is what Jesus was talking about), rape, child abuse, incest, masochism, or sadism would be not only sinful but also a sign of possible pathology. Between these extreme examples there is an almost infinite spectrum of fantasies that are more or less sinless and sinful, healthy and pathological. We are imperfect people with imperfect fantasies, sexual and otherwise. So we live by grace— thanking God for all that is good and life-giving, resting in for-giveness for all that is less than good, and praying to be healed of all that is unhealthy and life-degrading.

YOU ARE
DIVORCED OR WIDOWED AND
"SOMETHING" BEGINS TO DEVELOP

We've already written about the need to be cautious as a relation-ship begins to blossom. A special word is in order for those who have been married and now find themselves in a new relationship that could lead to another marriage.

There are two dangers. One is that you may be so badly scarred from your first marriage that you are reluctant to trust another man or woman. This alone is good reason to take it slow and easy the next time around. If you have found a good poten-tial partner, that person will understand your reluctance to rush into another marriage. We strongly urge you to seek the assis-tance of a professional counselor and your spiritual advisor. Go as an individual and go as a couple. Speak openly and candidly of your fears. Share with your new friend as much about your pre-vious relationship as your counselor deems advisable. If you have children, seek advice on how much they need to be drawn into the discussion.

The other danger is that you may have had a wonderful previ-ous marriage and may still be in such grief that you are not as ready for another marriage as you may think. Rushing blindly and hastily into another relationship could spell disaster. After the death of one's mate, it's not unusual to forget some of their negative qualities and magnify their good ones. One might easily burden a new marriage with expectations that are neither fair nor realistic. Again, investment in help from a professional counselor will be money well spent; you need all the help you can get before taking the plunge.

A NOTE ON CELIBACY

In the history of Christianity there is a long and honored tradition of celibacy. Some devote themselves to a religious order that requires it. But there are also laypersons who believe they can serve God and others better if they make a deliberate choice not to marry. These persons often learn to sublimate their sexual desires and to let those energies flow out in constructive ways to help others and enhance the life of a community. We can affirm all persons who make that choice.

But what happens to these persons as sexual beings, created like the rest of us? Do sexual feelings go away? If one sublimates them long enough, will they disappear? They may. But they most probably won't.

A male friend who devoted himself to celibacy early in his life told of the intense struggle he felt every time he met a beautiful woman on the street. He would quickly turn his eyes away. But even a fleeting glance was usually enough to set off a fire of desire to have an intimate relationship with a woman. When he confessed his sins, the transgression that loomed largest was what he believed to be inappropriate fantasies about women. Eventually, he left the celibate life, married a wonderful woman, and had the joy of sharing life with her as well as fathering three bright children.

We tell this story not to undermine the dedication of those who choose celibacy but to accent the fact that sexual feelings and thoughts do not go away just because one has made a choice to be single. In fact, it may well be that single persons, without the opportunity for a healthy expression of sexual urges in marriage, may struggle more with how to deal with sexual feelings than those who share life with a husband or wife.

FOR COUPLES WHO MAY MARRY

Let's devote a few paragraphs to those single years before people marry. As you read in the previous chapter, we hold to a traditional view: We believe that couples should wait until they're married before they engage in sexual intercourse. We don't set ourselves up as judges.

Having said this, we're not a couple of ostriches with our heads buried in the sand. We know what's going on out there. A group of pastors was asked to estimate what percentage of couples who came for counseling in preparation for marriage were already having sexual intercourse. The low estimate was 70 percent, the high 90 percent. In another setting a pastor from a small-town parish in Minnesota reported that she asked each couple who came to be married if they were engaging in sexual intercourse. Over a seven-year period it was 100 percent.

We realize that there are some, including biblical scholars, who believe that one cannot make a valid case for absolute abstinence from intercourse before marriage. We also recognize, as anthropologists and missionaries tell us, that premarital sexual mores vary greatly from one culture to another. And, furthermore, we don't want to sit in judgment over those couples who had no intention of "going too far," but who in a moment of passion engaged in genital sex, including occasions when it led to a pregnancy. Because it is difficult to wait, setting a date for marriage and then delaying it, for whatever reason, is not a good idea. Couples who find they have no choice but to delay their marriage will need to exercise special caution in saving for their marriage the unique intimacy that comes with sexual intercourse.

We base our case for abstinence from sexual intercourse prior to marriage on the theme that runs through this book—the foundation of a full, deep relationship is the best context for sexual fulfillment.

An illustration may help. We both love to garden. We understand the rhythm of growth in the plant world. A seed needs a good environment in which to germinate. A young seed needs the nourishment of water, sun, and nutrients from the soil in order to establish a good root system. Though unseen below the surface of the ground, these roots are absolutely critical to the plant's ability to flourish and, finally, bear a good harvest of food or a bright display of flowers.

That's the way it should be for a relationship that's building toward a good marriage. It's unthinkable to us that a young man should look at a woman with thoughts of "conquering" her sexually. Or that he should feel like a failure if he hasn't persuaded her to "go all the way" after a few dates. Contrariwise, it's equally as bizarre and pathetic that a young woman should think that she can "get her man" by making herself easily available for sexual intercourse. We're not suggesting for a moment that there's anything wrong with feeling sexual attraction for someone. It may be the first impulse that makes us inclined to like a certain person. And as a result of that initial attraction, many learn over time that they have been drawn to a wonderful person who makes a good mate.

But it also needs to be said that if it goes no deeper one can get stuck on a very superficial level of sexual attraction. A psychiatrist friend points out on the basis of his pragmatic experience that "having sex too soon slows the growth of the relationship" and that such couples often "fail to pay attention to important factors concerning shared philosophy of life, child rearing, and spirituality." Such persons soon discover—if not before marriage, certainly soon after—that a relationship focused on sex alone will soon wither and die.

So What Can We Do?

That's a fair question. A very fair question. And there is no easy answer. If we suggest that one should refrain from sexual intercourse, are we saying that "anything but" is all right? Some make a distinction between "intercourse" and "outercourse," which consists of all kinds of sexual activity short of penile penetration, and argue that this is all right. Some people believe they remain virgins so long as they do not have genital intercourse. While that may be technically true, we believe that a couple who focuses on "anything but" will be in danger of getting stuck on a plateau in their relationship.

Zits: *By Jerry Scott and Jim Borgman*

Reprinted with special permission of King Features Syndicate.

For starters, we recognize that the situation will vary from couple to couple. We both have friends who married after a very short acquaintance. For them the issue was not very large. Though a vanishing practice, we've also visited other cultures where the parents chose a mate. In some instances the couple did not meet until the day of their wedding. They tell us that they learn to love each other after they marry. There's no need to worry about sexual contact before one's wedding day.

But we live in a different setting. Radically different. Because both of us dated our wives for several years before marriage, we have some understanding of the dynamics of a relationship between two persons who love each other deeply and are moving toward the altar over a long period of time. We also know that couples now tend to marry later than was the case when we married.

Delaying marriage because of the need for more education or because of a desire to be more financially secure are factors that are moving upward the average age of marriage. And all of this when one is at the stage of maximum sexual interest!

Some Suggestions

This is a murky area, but we want to venture some suggestions:

First, as you become better acquainted, focus on the totality of your relationship. Do you share a broad range of interests? This will sustain you in marriage. Do you embrace a common faith, or at least a willingness to explore this area together? If you intend to make a grace-centered community an important part of your marriage, it will be imperative that you make some important decisions about this early in your relationship. Developing the habit of worshiping together before marriage will not only give you added incentive to discuss moral and spiritual values, but will help to lay a solid foundation for an active church involvement after marriage.

Are you intellectually compatible? We're not speaking about equal IQs or the same level of academic achievement. Your specific interests may vary. But do you find each other stimulating when you engage in conversation?

Do you enjoy the same kinds of people? Since they will likely be your friends after you marry, are they the kinds of persons both of you will enjoy for years to come?

Second, lean toward the side of caution in your physical relationship. Think about the consequences of a given action before you take the leap. Early in the relationship a good-night kiss will be as far as you'll want to go. As you deepen your trust and confidence in each other, you will feel free to embrace more tightly. Touching skin is very stimulating for both persons. Do it with caution. Keep asking yourselves, "Is this the right pace for us? Is what we're doing appropriate for this stage of our relationship?" If you sense you've gone too far, talk about it. Hard though it may be, have the good sense to back up a step or two when necessary.

As you approach engagement, you'll be thinking about commitment in a deeper sense. Although practices are changing and engagement, for some, may not hold the same degree of seriousness that it did a generation ago, we think it can still serve a very constructive purpose in moving toward marriage. Now you may find yourself thinking with excitement about your future mate when you're not together. Is it all right to fantasize about that person and even to engage in self-pleasuring while doing so? We think it is. Is it a good idea for a man to stroke, fondle, and kiss the breasts of his future mate? We think it better not to go this far. That will be a decision, however, to be made by each couple. Though there are those who claim they can do it, we think it's extremely difficult to stop at that point. For those who disagree, we urge caution with an understanding that this will be the limit. Is it appropriate to engage in stimulation of the genitals, either manually or orally? We don't think so.

Why not "go all the way"? Why do we urge caution? Why pace oneself? Among the many good reasons is that one cannot be certain, even after engagement, that there will be a wedding. Couples change their minds, even up to the last moment. Why not reserve for that very special one—that person with whom you will share life "until death parts us"—some of the most intimate aspects of a sexual relationship? When tempted, remember that deeds have consequences. Let your head and your heart, not your hormones, control your actions. Set clear limits and you may be surprised to discover you have great powers of self-control.

For Those Who Disagree with Us

What about couples who are unwilling to either postpone sexual fulfillment or experience it through self-pleasuring? We would still encourage them to refrain from genital sexual intercourse. In her book *Sex with Love: A Guide for Young People*, Eleanor Hamilton,

Ph.D., gives this advice to couples whose "sexuality is bursting for release and fulfillment together":

> At this point a thoughtless young man may try to persuade his partner to have sexual intercourse. This is a great mistake—sexual intercourse is simply not the *only* pleasurable sexual satisfaction nor the best training ground for ultimate artistry in sex.
>
> There is a way, however, that intelligent youth may express sexuality that is perfectly safe and perfectly adapted to his or her need. It is called noncoital petting to orgasm. The word *coitus* is another name for intercourse.
>
> So *noncoital* means sexually fulfilled without intercourse. Sophisticated lovers have known about this very satisfying way of sexual expression for centuries; . . . however, because of the persistence of folklore that labels intercourse "the only real thing," young people are deluded into thinking that if they are to know the ultimate they must have intercourse.
>
> Actually, mutual petting to orgasm is likely to be much more *satisfying* to the girl and equally satisfying for the boy—and it offers both boy and girl a safe and happily complete way to share their physical affection for each other. (38–39)

Because we believe it is best for dating couples to refrain from genital sexual activity, we have serious reservations concerning Dr. Hamilton's advice. But for those who refuse to heed our counsel, we commend what she encourages as an alternative that is preferable to intercourse.

To Those Who Insist on Intercourse

To dating couples who reject both our urging to abstain from all genital sexual activity and Dr. Hamilton's recommended alternative to intercourse, we say, "Whatever you do, don't create an unwanted pregnancy or give, or receive, a sexually transmitted disease." We and Dr. Hamilton agree that dating couples should not have sexual intercourse and wish that all would heed our wisdom. But to those who won't, we say, "Never have intercourse without protection against pregnancy and disease." Contraceptive pills provide significant, but not perfect, protection against pregnancy when taken as prescribed. They provide no protection against sexually transmitted diseases. Therefore, unless a couple has never been involved sexually with anyone else, the use of a condom during every act of intercourse is absolutely necessary. This will provide significant, but again less than perfect, protection against both pregnancy and disease.

Although it doesn't sound very romantic, we believe that persons who are being tempted to enter a sexual relationship are fully justified in asking their potential sex partners to be tested for sexually transmitted diseases and if they have had previous sexual encounters to offer to be tested. Because detectable antibodies aren't immediately present, such tests cannot guarantee the absence of HIV, the virus that causes AIDS. If, however, there has been sufficient time since exposure, it can be detected, as can the presence of herpes, gonorrhea, and syphilis. If someone is unwilling to go through such testing, it is a significant indication that the couple is insufficiently committed to have sexual intercourse.

We are aware that some will strongly object to our discussing any alternatives to total abstinence from genital sexual activity. We agree with their goal but think they are being unrealistic. At a time when surveys indicate that the majority of high school students have had intercourse before graduation, and that this activity generates thousands of unwanted pregnancies and sexually transmitted diseases each year, we believe that we need to do more than tell teenagers and young adults to "just say no!"

We applaud those who are saying no, and we are grateful for reports of those who wear the kind of "promise rings" that tell their friends and dating partners they intend to refrain from sex until marriage. At the same time, we see our advice to be like that from a parent to a newly licensed teenaged driver: "Please drive carefully. Don't speed or drive recklessly. And, whatever you do, buckle your seat belt!" We don't think that urging seat-belt use encourages reckless driving; nor do we believe that properly presented discussion of alternatives to intercourse and means of pregnancy and disease prevention encourages promiscuity.

Proper presentation focuses on wisdom, not legalism. Laying down the law often prompts rebellion. Perhaps that's part of what the apostle Paul had in mind when he said, "When the commandment came, sin revived and I died, and the very commandment that promised life proved to be death to me" (Rom. 7:9-10). We have heard people boast of their sinful sexual conquests. We have never heard anyone boast of being a fool! Exploitative sexual activity at whatever age is not just sinful, it is stupid, and in the long run it leads not to the joy of gratitude but to the misery of regret. Parental and pastoral counsel with teenagers needs to be bluntly realistic in emphasizing this fact.

MOST OF ALL—WALK IN FAITH

Much more could be said. But this final word seems in order: Single or attached, we should all seek to walk by faith. Take as your daily guide the promise in Psalm 32:8—"I will instruct you and teach you in the way you should go; I will counsel you with my eye upon you." Christians believe that God is interested in all of life, including single life. Let it be your prayer that you will be sensitive to the guidance of God's Spirit as you search for fulfillment and meaning in your life. If your search leads to a lifelong relationship, well and good. But if not, God has no intention that your life should be arid and dull. Quite to the contrary, God wills that you enjoy it to the fullest.

QUESTIONS & ANSWERS

Q: I am a tenth grader and have been doing well in school and at home, but now I am in big trouble. About a week ago my mother somehow figured out that I masturbate, and she gave me a big lecture about evil and the dangers of "abusing myself" and told me that as a Christian I should save myself for marriage. I am sure she told my dad, but he hasn't said anything, which is probably good, since I am too embarrassed to talk to him about it. I have tried to follow my mother's advice, but have already failed at that. Is masturbation really as bad as she says it is, and if so, what can I do to stop? Our pastor preached a sermon some time ago about how God knows all our secret sins. I thought he was talking about me and I really tried to stop, but was never able to for more than a few days. I once heard someone say that when we are tempted sexually we should take a cold shower or work real hard so that we'd fall asleep as soon as we go to bed. I tried that and it didn't work! Do you have any advice?

A: When we were your age we also heard stories about how terrible masturbation is. Some years later we learned that it is normal and harmless. Now many Christian counselors are saying that it is healthy and good and that parents and pastors should tell their kids it's okay and refrain from saying things that make them feel ashamed or guilty about it. Many years ago a Roman Catholic priest told one of us that he believed that "masturbation is God's gift to the celibate." We would suggest that it is also God's gift to the celibate—that is, those not married. We have come to believe that it is better to think of it as God's gift and not a temptation of the devil. That's why we prefer the term "self-pleasuring" rather than "masturbation." Masturbation carries with it too much negative baggage. If teenagers, and adults, would think of self-pleasuring as God's gift, they probably would masturbate a lot less, enjoy it a lot more, and be grateful for it instead of guilty about it.

Trying hard not to do something often makes things worse. Suppose, for example, that someone tells you, "Whatever you do, never think about monkeys!" If you try hard to follow that advice, there will be monkeys in your mind all day long. If nobody had ever told you not to do it, you would almost never think about monkeys. Your parents are well intentioned, but in this case we think your mother is wrong in her scolding, and your dad is wrong in his silence. They may even believe the Bible condemns self-pleasuring. Let us assure you that there is not a word about it in Scripture. One passage speaks of spilling the seed on the ground but that is about evading a cultural responsibility, not about self-pleasuring (see Gen. 38:6-10 and Deut. 25:5-10).

If you think it would be helpful, you are welcome to share our thoughts with your mom and dad. If you think that would just make things worse, we encourage you to take our thoughts to heart and to discreetly try to avoid any further confrontation with your parents. Whatever you choose to do, remember that nothing you have done or can ever do will stop God from loving you. As you live in God's grace, you will discover that sex is only one of God's many good gifts and that there are lots of other things to which you can give your attention. When that happens, sex will have its proper place in your life, and you won't have to always be preoccupied with it.

Q: I am embarrassed to tell you what I am embarrassed about. I heard Jay Leno making jokes one night about men who weren't very well endowed, and I had the feeling he was making fun of me. When we take showers after gym class, I can't help but notice that a lot of the guys are bigger than I am. Nobody has ever said anything, but it still bothers me a lot and I wonder if there is something wrong with me. Everything seems to work okay, if you know what I mean, but I still wonder if I should see a doctor or get hormone treatments or something. What do you think?

A: We think that it is exceedingly likely that you are 100 percent normal. We, too, have been in a lot of locker-room showers and observed these same differences that cause some men to feel macho and others inferior. We have never done any research on this subject, but we have seen reports of the research of others that reveal a couple of things you should remember. One is that while there are significant differences in the size of relaxed penises, there is much less difference when they are erect. Note, for example, that most condoms are the same size. The other is that size has very little, if anything, to do with sexual satisfaction for either a man or a woman.

We hope that this helps to relieve your anxiety and that you won't need to spend any more time worrying about it. If you still think that you are somehow abnormal, we encourage you to consult with your family physician or a urology specialist, who will likely give you further assurance that you are perfectly normal.

Q: My boyfriend and I began having sexual relations a couple of months ago. We know that it is wrong, but now that we have gone all the way, it seems we can't stop. Sometimes we even promise each other that we won't do it again, but before the date is over our promises are broken.

We love each other and have talked about getting married some day, but I am only fifteen and he is sixteen, so that can't happen for a long time.

To be totally honest, our sexual relations are very satisfying for both of us, so even though we are trying to stop, I am not sure that either of us really wants to. The way things have been going the last couple of months, I am sure we won't be able to keep on dating and not have sex until we are old enough to get married. If we should die, do you think God would condemn us to hell? What do you think we should do?

A: First of all, we want to assure you that even when our sins make God sad, they never stop God from loving us. God loves you and wants what is best for you. God didn't give us the Ten Commandments to keep us from having fun, but to help us live in ways that are best for ourselves and for others and also to remind us that we always need God's forgiveness. Whatever you do, never stop trusting God's love and forgiveness. When we rest in God's abounding grace, we don't need to worry about being condemned to hell.

At the same time, we encourage you to pray for strength to do what is right. We think that the best thing for you would be to stop having sexual relations until you are married. We think that's possible through the grace of God. But as we hear your story, we recognize that it's not probable. Therefore, we encourage you first of all to never do anything that will cause an unwanted pregnancy or give each other a sexually transmitted disease. That means that you should never have sexual relations without using a condom. We strongly encourage you to discuss contraception with your doctor or school nurse and to take no chances.

Protection against disease also means that you will be faithful to each other and never have sexual relations with anyone else. You hope to be married some day and should, therefore, live now as if you had already taken the vows of marriage.

We also encourage you to explore ways of satisfying each other without intercourse by caressing each other with your hands. Some couples have found this to be a mutually satisfying way of saving intercourse for marriage. It may be a way for you to abstain from intercourse until you are married.

We want what is best for you and pray that grace will abound to enable you to live in ways that lead to the maximum of gratitude and a minimum of regret. God bless you always.

Q: I once heard one of you speak positively about what you called "sexual self-fulfillment." Since that has been, and in fact still is, a part of my life, I would be glad to be persuaded that it's really okay, but I still have my doubts. I understand, as you went on to say, that there is nothing about it in the Bible, but then I remember what Jesus said about looking at a woman lustfully. He said that's committing adultery in our hearts.

Maybe some people can indulge in self-pleasuring without sexual fantasies, but I haven't had much success at that. It is as if my hormones and my imagination gang up on me, and I confess to enjoying both my imaginative adventures and my physical sensations. But then I remember what Jesus said about lustful looking and I feel terribly guilty. That is especially true when a sexy picture, and it doesn't have to be pornographic, has stimulated my imagination. What about those fantasies? Am I guilty of committing adultery in my head if not my heart? If I am guilty, will God forgive me when I keep on sinning over and over again?

A: We will respond to your last question first. Jesus teaches us to forgive seventy times seven, which is a way of saying that we are never to stop forgiving, and assures us that that is the way God forgives, and that nothing we have ever done or can ever do will stop God from loving us. There are sins that are more frequent than lustful looking. We are proud, greedy, and excessively self-preoccupied in sinful self-centeredness every moment of every day, but in gracious, forgiving mercy, God continues to love us every moment. We are not to take such grace as permission to sin, but we are to live in constant remembrance of the fact, as Luther emphasized, that we are simultaneously sinful and forgiven.

Now, concerning those fantasies: We all have healthful and normal sexual desires and fantasies that are not sinful, and it is likely true that we also have fantasies, sexual and otherwise, that are sinful. For example, it may be greedily sinful to fantasize over what we would do if we won ten million dollars, but it might not be sinful to imagine ourselves driving the new car or living in the new home that we really need.

Similarly with sex—we have God-given sexual desires and we are created for sexual fulfillment. Would anyone ever marry if we didn't fantasize about the fulfillment, including sexual pleasure, we imagine marriage will bring? We doubt that this is what Jesus was thinking of when he spoke about adulterous, lustful looking. Some Biblical scholars believe that what Jesus was really condemning was the desire to possess another man's wife and that this sin has more to do with covetousness than with normal sexual desires and fantasies.

Our ability to fantasize is a gift from God. Our lives would be far poorer and in many ways less interesting and exciting without our God-given capacity to imagine and daydream. There is no doubt a fine line exists between healthful and hurtful fantasies and between those that are sinless and sinful, but we don't think that God who has created these capacities condemns them all. Therefore, without being able to scan the specific fantasies of your mind, we guess that they are probably more harmless than hurtful, and that they may even be more helpful than harmless. They may even be God's gift for your life fulfillment.

There are verses in the Bible that tell us, in effect, that we can eat anything we can thank God for (see 1 Tim. 4:3). The same is true of our fantasies—if they bring joy and meaning to our lives, we can be grateful instead of guilty. As Paul goes on to say to Timothy, "For everything created by God is good, and nothing is to be rejected, provided it is received with thanksgiving" (1 Tim. 4:4).

Q: I wonder if there is something wrong with me. I have never had a sexual relationship with anyone, and I don't indulge in what some call solitary sex. I have a great job, lots of friends, and am involved in a number of extremely satisfying volunteer activities. In all honesty, I am living a contented and joyful life. So what's the problem? My problem springs from all the media hype about sex. It's almost everywhere. It appears to be the main thing that a lot of people think about, and I think about it hardly at all! It makes me wonder if I got shortchanged on sex hormones.

If the right person comes along, I'd be glad to be happily married and to have a family someday, but that is certainly not because I'm starving for sex. If marriage doesn't happen, I don't think I'll be burdened with grief. I'm having a great time now and don't see why I can't go on having a lot of life fulfillment without marriage and without sex. Isn't that okay?

A: If it's okay with you, it's certainly okay with us. We have often said that sex is good but it's not God, and we wonder if the way a lot of people worship sex is not only out of sync with reality but is also a kind of idolatry.

We believe that life-giving sexuality takes many forms, including satisfying and sometimes sanctified sublimation. That is, instead of being expressed in specific genital activity, it is the creative force that finds its expression in hundreds of ways, such as music and art, friendship and sports, meaningful work and life-giving service. You sound to us like a sane and sensible person, and we encourage you to ignore the sexual hype and to keep focused on all of the good things that give meaning to your life and which, from the sounds of it, also give a lot of joy and meaning to others.

Q: I am a thirty-five-year-old virgin who has been saving myself for marriage. I was in a serious relationship with a man, but that has now ended and the prospects for marriage seem dim.

After our breakup I told a good friend that "I don't want to die as a virgin" and she, to my embarrassment, shared this with her husband, who told his wife that he would be glad to solve my problem. When she didn't go for that idea, he told her that he has a single friend who would be glad to help me out. We have now dated a couple of times, and he seems like a nice guy, but I am sure I'll never marry him. We have had no sexual involvement, but he has hinted at his willingness to be helpful. The idea both tempts and scares me. Do you think it would be wrong and foolish for me to accept his "helpfulness"?

A: In one word, our answer is "yes!" We think it would be both wrong and foolish and also that you would likely find such a sexual experience unsatisfying and regrettable. Maybe it won't mean much coming from a couple of long-married men, but we think that there are worse things in life than to die as a virgin and that one of them is to have empty and regrettable sexual experiences. To speak frankly, we think that you can have a lot better sex in solitude than you would have in a superficial fling with this fellow, however nice he may be.

Our wish for you is that you will yet find a relationship to which you can truly give yourself in love and commitment. In the meantime, we encourage you to find emotional fulfillment in the depth of nonsexual friendships, and your specific sexual fulfillment in self-pleasuring. There are some people who would tell you that they believe you will, in your singleness, be experiencing the best of both the emotional and sexual worlds.

Q: Our son and daughter will soon be teenagers, and we are already beginning to worry about how they will deal with the sexual temptations that are likely to confront them during adolescence. Beginning years ago, we have tried to honestly answer their sexual questions. We are grateful that they have received some responsible sex education in school and in their confirmation classes. We wonder, what more should we do now?

A: On the basis of what you have shared with us, we commend you, your church, and your children's school for the sex education they have received thus far. It sounds as if you have all done well. We also call your attention to the books for children and teenagers that are suggested in the resources at the end of this book.

A more specific example of how you might personally instruct your children can be found in a long letter from a "North Dakota Mom" that first appeared in "Dear Abby" on December 11, 1991, and was reprinted February 22, 2000. It describes how one concerned and courageous mother dealt with her thirteen-year-old daughter. We weren't as candid and direct with our children and are sure that many parents will be uncomfortable about being this concrete and confrontational with their sons and daughters, but we believe that some frank conversation along these lines is to be affirmed. Therefore, please ponder this example and apply it as you are able.

DEAR ABBY:

I wrote to you in June about my 13-year-old daughter. (I told you she was getting dangerously close to the boyfriend she had been seeing morning, noon, and night.)

I took your advice and spoke to her about sex. I purchased at the local drugstore several forms of birth control (condoms, contraceptive sponge, and vaginal suppositories). I also bought something called a "teen pack." It contained several trial-size items introducing young females to such things as tampons, maxi pads, shaving lotion, and razors for shaving legs. When I got home, I invited my daughter to join me at the kitchen table. My husband was working late that night, so it was a perfect opportunity for girl talk.

I lined up the contraceptive devices on the table. I gave her the teen pack, telling her that all the items in that package were things that we had previously discussed. Then I pointed to the other items that we needed to talk about.

I carefully explained to her that now that she had become a young woman having a monthly period, she could become pregnant if she had sex. I then told her that I was in no way condoning sex in someone as young as she but that I wanted her to be informed. I took each product and explained how it was used, and showed her the directions and how to check the expiration date on the product. After that, I opened each package and let her touch the device, examine it and ask questions.

I made sure that she was aware that even if she was on the birth control pill, it would not prevent sexually transmitted diseases, such as AIDS. I told her that safe sex with condoms could not guarantee the prevention of pregnancy and disease, and the only way to ensure not getting a sexually transmitted disease was not to have sex.

I then took the remaining products and placed them in a box in her bathroom closet. I told her I would not check the box, but if she ever felt a need to experiment, they would be there. I stressed that she could always come to me before making any decisions that would change her life forever.

I made some important points to her that truly hit home: I pointed out that she was too young to obtain a driver's license, too young to drink, too young to get a job, and too young to be responsible for the life of another human being. I reminded her that if she were to have a child, her education and social life would cease until such time that she could afford a baby-sitter.

Abby, I realize this letter is long, but I wanted you to know how I dealt with this issue. After our talk, my daughter has been a different person!

I trust my daughter, and your advice was a big help in dealing with a very difficult situation. I realize that I have a long way to go in completing the journey through her teen years, but I believe that we, as a family, will survive.

—North Dakota Mom

DEAR MOM:

Thank you for writing. Every daughter should have a mother like you!

Taken from DEAR ABBY *column by Abigail Van Buren. Copyright © 2000 Universal Press Syndicate. Reprinted with permission.*

We can debate some of the specifics in that mother's letter, but we have no doubt that such an approach is far more likely to encourage responsible sexual behavior than is an authoritarian "Just say no!"

Q: I am a forty-year-old divorcée with a good job and no immediate interest in marrying again. I have a couple of male friends whose company I enjoy and who are happy to help satisfy my sexual needs. Since everyone is happy with this arrangement, I don't see that we are hurting anyone. Is there anything wrong with my present way of life?

A: If you had said that you had one male friend with whom you had a relationship that was the moral and emotional equivalent of marriage, you might have evoked our blessing along with our strong encouragement to seal that relationship with marriage at the earliest possible date. But when you speak of "a couple of male friends" we think that you are traveling down a dangerous road that will eventually cause grief for your friends and especially for yourself.

From our perspective, sex is not just another recreational activity like golf or playing cards that we can enjoy with almost anybody. There is something special, even sacramental, about it that finds its fulfillment in a relationship of caring and commitment. Your relationships with both of these men may involve some caring but certainly no commitment. They sound emotionally superficial, and that means that in the long run they will be sexually superficial as well. Therefore, we encourage you to end your sexual involvement with both of them. If you later become serious enough with one of the them to become truly committed, that will be soon enough to resume the sexual relationship, along with arrangements for marriage.

5 | SEXUAL FULFILLMENT
WHILE LIVING TOGETHER

WE HAVE BEEN INVOLVED IN DOZENS of forums and discussion groups concerning sexual issues. After hearing our strong affirmation of marriage, a participant often asks, "What about sexual relationships apart from marriage?" The questioner is often a parent who goes on to tell of an unmarried son or daughter who is living with someone. The parents don't like this arrangement and wonder what, if anything, they should say. The live-in couple is now coming for a visit. The parents don't want them sleeping together in their home but also don't want to create a crisis. The person ends by asking, "What should we do?"

In the early years of our ministries we sometimes met with couples who had "jumped the gun" sexually speaking and who met with us to plan an as-soon-as-possible "shotgun wedding." Only rarely did we meet a couple bold enough to tell us that they were living together prior to marriage. Have times ever changed!

In response to such questions and concerns, we confess to being alarmed and distressed by the statistics. The National Marriage Project of Rutgers University reports:

> Between 1960 and 1998 . . . the number of unmarried couples in America increased by close to 1,000 percent. . . . It is estimated that about a quarter of unmarried women aged 25 to 39 are currently living with a partner and about half have lived at some time with an unmarried partner. Over half of all first marriages are now preceded by living together, compared to virtually none earlier in the century. (16)

CAN COHABITATING RELATIONSHIPS BE LIFE-GIVING?

We have described life-giving sex both in terms of procreation of new life and the re-creation of the lovers' lives. When relationships apart from marriage result in pregnancies, they are, in this sense, life-giving, and the children born of such unions are the gift of God. But because many of these pregnancies are unwanted and result in either abortion or in the birth of children who are regarded as more of a burden than a blessing, it is obvious that we cannot describe every pregnancy as joyfully life-giving.

But what if disciplined use of contraception prevents unwanted pregnancy? Can nonmarital, and even extramarital, sexual relationships be truly life-giving for the couples involved? These are the basic questions we seek to address in this chapter. As we wrestle with the reality of heterosexual sex apart from marriage, we ask ourselves, "Is life-giving sexual fulfillment possible in such relationships?"

Our Present Conviction

After years of struggling with this question, our present conviction is that such fulfillment may be possible, but only in relationships that are, in effect, the moral and emotional equivalent of marriage. We believe that, apart from such a relationship, sexual involvement results in more grief than gratitude.

Please note that we do not encourage couples who are in such "equivalent of marriage" relationships to become sexually involved. Both of us are grateful for the gift of coming to our marriages with this new and exciting experience to share with our wives. We do not condemn couples who are sexually involved in "equivalent of marriage" relationships, but neither do we encourage it. We believe that premature sexual activity often short-circuits a relationship and keeps a couple from really getting to know each other.

WHAT IS MARRIAGE?

Having spoken of relationships that are the moral and emotional equivalent of marriage, we must stop a moment and answer the question, "What is marriage?" Some will say that this is a dumb question! People are either single or married. The married ones have gotten a marriage license, had a wedding ceremony of some kind, and had it recorded with the state so that it is a matter of public record. It's as simple as that and there is no need to have lengthy discussion of silly questions like "What is marriage?"

Alfred North Whitehead said that we are to "seek simplicity and distrust it." We have also heard that "there are simple answers to profound questions and most of them are wrong!" We believe that both statements apply to the question "What is marriage?" especially when considered from a Christian, biblical perspective. There is no account in the Bible of anyone going to a county courthouse to get a marriage license. The Bible tells us that King Solomon had 700 wives and 300 concubines, and we can be sure he didn't promise each one to "keep only unto her" for the rest of his life (see 1 Kings 11:3). The Bible speaks often of husbands and wives, and sometimes of weddings, but it doesn't contain a model wedding ceremony or specific definition of marriage. Therefore, the Christian church throughout the centuries and throughout the world has wrestled seriously with the definition of marriage, and has blessed marital practices that have varied considerably from age to age and place to place.

The church has generally rejected sexual involvement of any kind before marriage. We are old enough to remember a time when a respected church leader said that it was okay for engaged couples to hold hands, but that they should refrain from kissing until the pastor invited them to kiss each other during their wedding. The limited sex education that we received from the church in those days was not that restricted, but it was certainly clear that we were expected to refrain from intercourse prior to marriage. Now, with literally millions of couples choosing to live together without marriage and many more making no secret of their sexual involvement, the church has been compelled to ask not only "What constitutes marriage?" but also "What is going on here?"

For centuries the church has adapted to various forms of governmental regulation of marriage. In the United States, clergy are designated agents of the state when they perform marriages. In many other countries, couples are legally married by an officer of the state and those who desire it then have their marriage blessed at a wedding in the church.

The Essentials of Marriage

In spite of all these differences, there are essential characteristics that we believe witness to what constitutes marriage from a Christian perspective. At the heart of the marriage ceremony are the vows of love, commitment, and faithfulness declared by a couple to each other and witnessed by representatives of the community. In our tradition couples actually marry each other, and the clergy person or judge and the official witnesses are only witnesses whose signatures on a document recorded by the state provides proof that this couple is legally married.

Nevertheless, as the practice of the Roman Catholic Church concerning annulments makes clear, a couple can go through such a ceremony and, in effect, remain unmarried. If, for example, the relationship is never sexually consummated or if it can be shown that the vows were made under duress or in a situation of deception and deceit, the church can declare that there was no marriage. Such a couple is still married in the eyes of the state but not of the church. Even though it does not permit divorce, Roman Catholic couples whose marriages have been annulled are free to get legal termination of marriage since in the eyes of the church no marriage ever existed.

Relationships Equivalent to Marriage

Openness to the possibility of faithful, life-giving, God-affirming relationships apart from legal or ecclesiastical marriage is light-years away from the "if it feels good, do it" philosophy. These couples are mature persons who have less formally but no less sincerely shared vows of commitment with each other and have witnessed to this fact by telling family and friends that they are not just "shacking up" but have entered a relationship they intend to be lifelong. Living by this standard would eliminate genital sexual activity in relationships that lack the four qualities of mutual love, mutual respect, mutual openness, and mutual faithfulness that add up to mutual commitment as discussed in our chapter on marriage.

To test for such a relationship, a couple should ask themselves and each other some significant questions, such as: "Are we really committed to lifelong faithfulness to each other?"; "Do we trust each other enough to have a joint checking account?"; "Do we have sufficient care and respect for each other, as well as respect for life, to assume responsibility for a child that might be conceived in spite of our contraceptive efforts?" We believe that they should also give serious consideration to our warning that sexual relations may short-circuit rather than enhance their relationship.

All of these concerns relate to the basic question we ask all cohabiting couples who believe themselves to be in relationships that are the equivalent of marriage: "Why don't you have a wedding?" There may sometimes be valid reasons for not doing so, but we believe that marriage, when rightly understood, is a gift and blessing to be received and not, as some couples fear, a burden that may undermine or even destroy their wonderful relationship. There is surely some truth in what Dietrich Bonhoeffer once said: "It is not your love that sustains the marriage, but from now on, the marriage that sustains your love." We understand his point. Marriage itself, with its daily routines and commitments, helps a couple to maintain their love for each other. Having said that, we also believe that love for each other, including physical attraction, helps to sustain a marriage. Our marriages are sustained by love; but there have also been times when our love has been sustained by our marriages.

CONSIDER THE SOCIAL SCIENCE EVIDENCE

We strongly encourage all couples who are living together without marriage, or are thinking of doing so, to ponder carefully the comprehensive review of research that was recently published by Rutgers University. (Specific information is included in the appendix of resources.)

The Executive Summary and Conclusion of the Rutgers' study "Should We Live Together? What Young Adults Should Know About Cohabitation before Marriage" presents these findings:

> According to surveys, most young people say it is a good idea to live with a person before marrying. But a careful review of the available social science evidence suggests that living together is not a good way to prepare for marriage or to avoid divorce. What's more, it shows that the rise in cohabitation is not a positive family trend. Cohabiting unions tend to weaken the institution of marriage and pose clear and present dangers for women and children. Specifically, the research indicates that: Living together before marriage increases the risk of breaking up after marriage.
>
> Living together outside of marriage increases the risk of domestic violence for women, and the risk of physical and sexual abuse for children. Unmarried couples have lower levels of happiness and well being than married couples. (1–2)

The Executive Summary goes on to state:

We recognize the larger social and cultural trends that make cohabiting relationships attractive to many young adults today. Unmarried cohabitation is not likely to go away. Given this reality [one] purpose of this paper is to guide thinking on the question: "Should we live together?" We offer four principles that may help. These principles may not be the last words on the subject, but they are consistent with the available evidence and seem most likely to help never-married young adults avoid painful losses in their love lives and achieve satisfying and long-lasting relationships and marriage.

Consider not living together at all before marriage.

Cohabitation appears not to be helpful and may be hurtful as a trial for marriage. There is no evidence that if you decide to cohabit before marriage that you will have a stronger marriage than those that don't live together and some evidence suggests that if you live together before marriage, you are more likely to break up after marriage. Cohabitation is probably least harmful (though not necessarily helpful) when it is prenuptial, when both partners are definitely planning to marry, have formally announced their engagement and have picked the wedding date.

Do not make a habit of cohabiting.

Beware of the dangers of multiple living together experiences, both for your own sense of well being and for your chances of establishing a strong lifelong partnership. Contrary to popular wisdom, you do not learn to have better relationships from multiple failed cohabiting relationships. In fact, multiple cohabiting is a strong predictor of the failure of future relationships.

Limit cohabitation to the shortest possible period of time.

The longer you live together, . . . the more likely it is that the low-commitment ethic of cohabitation will take hold, the opposite of what is required for a successful marriage.

Do not cohabit if children are involved.

Children need and should have parents who are committed to staying together over the long term. Cohabiting parents break up at a much higher rate than married parents and the effects of a break-up can be devastating and often long-lasting. Moreover, children living in cohabiting unions are at higher risk of sexual abuse and physical violence, including lethal violence, than are children living with married parents. (1–3)

A concluding paragraph of the study reports:

In place of institutionalizing cohabitation, in our opinion, we should be trying to revitalize marriage—not along classic male-dominant lines but along modern egalitarian lines. Particularly helpful in this regard would be educating young people about marriage from the early school years onward, getting them to make the wisest choices in their lifetime mate, and stressing the importance of long-term commitment to marriages. Such an educational venture would build on the fact that a huge majority of our nation's young people still express the strong desire to be in a long-term monogamous marriage. (14)

Some are sure to regard the reservations of a couple of retired bishops concerning cohabitation as hopelessly outmoded and out-of-date. But we hope that none will ignore the convictions of these respected social scientists.

QUESTIONS & ANSWERS

Q: I was divorced several years ago following a difficult marriage. I have a good job and am able to provide well for myself and my two children, who are now away at college. During the last couple of years I have developed a relationship with a wonderful man who has also been divorced. He, too, has a responsible position and faithfully provides for his former wife and their children.

Several of our friends have encouraged us to get married, but we think there are good reasons for not doing so, at least not at this time. For one thing, he is a Roman Catholic and is deeply committed to his church. He can't be remarried in his church without first getting an annulment, which he doesn't want to do and thinks he probably wouldn't get if he were totally honest about his previous marriage. After having come through difficult marriages, we are a bit wary of marrying again. We have thought seriously about living together without marriage and know that that would be terribly upsetting to some members of both of our families. We are deeply in love and have promised to be faithful to each other and are now what might be called "an intimate dating couple." That intimacy does include sexual relations.

We have talked and prayed about this and believe that we are being very responsible, but we are still not altogether comfortable about it. Do you think that what we are doing is wrong? What would you advise?

A: Confronted with such concerns, we are grateful that we are not directive counselors who feel compelled to provide specific, final answers to every question. We agonize with you and feel both your sense of responsibility and your sense of discomfort with the arrangement you have worked out.

We think it would be best for you to be legally married. Have you discussed this possibility with a compassionate Roman Catholic priest? Is there any way for you to be married and for him to continue full participation in the life of his church? If that is not possible, are you open to the possibility of having a religious service in which you would share vows of love, faithfulness, and commitment with each other and would, in effect, be married in the sight of God but not legally?

If that is not a live option, are you open to telling your families and close friends that you have made such vows of commitment to each other and that you consider your relationship to be what we like to call "the moral and emotional equivalent of marriage"? If you do not have that degree of commitment we fear that you may have more reasons to feel uncomfortable than to feel responsible, but, we remind ourselves and you, the decision is yours and not ours. We know that God loves you and wills for you joy and life in fullness. May grace abound to guide you to live in ways that lead to an abundance of gratitude and a minimum of regret. Thank you for sharing your concerns with us. We encourage you to pursue them further in conversation with each other and with a compassionate counselor. God bless you always.

Q: Our daughter and her "friend" have been living together for about six months. They live several hundred miles from us and we haven't seen them since this happened. Our telephone conversations have been frequent but strained. We have told our daughter that we love and will never reject her, but we have also let her know that we don't approve of their living together when they are not married.

We are having a twenty-fifth wedding anniversary celebration in a couple of months and are trying to decide what to do. Should we invite only our daughter? Should we invite them both and treat them as if they were married? We have a big house and there is room for them to stay with us, but it would be upsetting for us to have them sleeping together under our roof. Do you think that it would be right for us to ask them to sleep in different bedrooms? What should we do if they tell us that is silly and refuse to do so? Do we then tell them to find a motel? Whatever happens, we don't want to do anything that will make her feel that she is rejected, and we certainly don't want to create a scene that will disrupt our happy celebration. What do you think we should do?

A: You have asked a lot of very difficult questions to which we can't give any clear and simple answers. If it is any comfort to you, be assured there are thousands of parents who are struggling with the same concerns.

Perhaps the best we can do is to suggest that you try to project yourselves into the future and to do what you think you will be grateful for five to ten years from now. None of us can be sure about that, but we think you will be thankful then for having invited both of them and for treating them in "almost" every way as if they were married. The "almost" relates to their sleeping together under your roof. We hope that you have the kind of relationship with your daughter that will enable you to have a candid conversation during which you confess your feelings in this regard. You may even acknowledge that they may think this is silly and old-fashioned. Ask her how she and her friend would feel about that. If she says that it will be okay, make up the beds in separate rooms and say no more about it. If she says they won't do that, you can kindly suggest that you would prefer they would stay at a motel. If she says that they won't attend the celebration unless they can sleep together in her parental home, you will have an exceedingly difficult decision to make. If it comes to that, we think that you are more likely to be grateful in the future for graciously, even though reluctantly, permitting them to sleep together.

If your daughter's relationship eventually leads to marriage, all of this will appear quite differently than it does today. If their relationship does not last, your daughter will have the memory of a time when you disagreed with her way of life but supported her with your unconditional love.

6 | SEXUAL FULFILLMENT IN SAME-SEX RELATIONSHIPS

A STRAIGHT LOOK AT A COMPLICATED ISSUE

WE KNEW LITTLE ABOUT HOMOSEXUALITY and didn't have a clear understanding of sexual orientation until well into adulthood. We grew up thinking that everyone was, like ourselves, sexually attracted to persons of the other sex. After our first known and direct contact with homosexual persons in the mid-1960s, it still took a long time for us to recognize and begin to understand that they were as sexually and affectionately attracted to persons of the same sex as we were to those of the opposite sex.

The issue of civil rights for homosexual persons came to the forefront in Minnesota in the mid-1970s, when the city of St. Paul was confronted with a referendum that would give equal rights to homosexual persons. Both sides sought the advice and support of religious leaders in the community. We endorsed the proposal. We soon learned, however, that anyone who spoke out in favor of it was stepping into a very incendiary arena. Strongly worded letters, indeed vitriolic letters, streamed to our desks, as well as to others who endorsed the proposal. We knew that this was an issue that would demand our attention in the years to come.

GETTING TO KNOW
HOMOSEXUAL PERSONS

We both determined to read as widely as possible on the subject. Some books and articles branded gay and lesbian persons as immoral and destined for eternal damnation. Others affirmed homosexuality as a gift from God to be celebrated. And between those poles were a plethora of opinions.

We also decided to get to know more homosexual persons firsthand and soon encountered something we had never before experienced: the witness of Christ-confessing gay and lesbian persons. They became our teachers and asked for our understanding. This moving testimony began to correct our misunderstanding and change our attitudes. We are convinced that these kinds of encounters are essential in coming to an intelligent and compassionate understanding of homosexuality.

Typical of those early contacts was a meeting in the late 1970s with a group who called themselves "Lutherans Concerned." The recollection of the evening is vivid. It was held in an old mansion on Summit Avenue in St. Paul. Two friendly young men were at the front door to greet everyone who attended. It was quiet in the house. One had to wonder if there would be others at this gathering. That uncertainty soon evaporated. Seated in a circle in the living room were about twenty young men. There was stony silence in the room. As we joined the circle, we saw some familiar faces. Across the room sat a young man who was the son of one of our most able and well-known pastors. As the evening unfolded at least one other man identified himself as the son of another respected pastor. Suddenly the quest for better understanding took on a very personal dimension.

Everyone in the circle was uneasy at first. But as they introduced themselves one by one and told their stories, it became apparent that they were very normal, sensitive young men. More important, one had to be impressed by their love for Christ and the church.

They invited questions from their guests.

"Can you change?" That brought nervous laughter, followed by painful stories of vain attempts at it: healing services, expensive and extensive counseling, intense prayer for change, longing to be different. But, finally, they told story after story of coming to peace with a decision to accept themselves—indeed, to affirm themselves—as homosexual persons.

"Were you abused?" More nervous laughter. None had been sexually abused.

"Did you have poor relationships with your parents, especially your mother?" No, not one of them could point to that as a cause for being gay. One told of having seven siblings, all of them straight. The same mother and father, the same environment, yet, for reasons he could not explain, he was gay.

"Parents worry that you'll 'corrupt' their children. Is that a legitimate concern?" More nervous chuckles. One who identified himself as an elementary teacher said that taking advantage of a child would be the last thing he would ever do. Others reminded us of something straight folks sometimes overlook, namely that children are no more at risk from homosexual teachers or leaders than they are from straight ones.

MOVING ACROSS THE SPECTRUM

Not long after that St. Paul meeting there was a conference in San Francisco sponsored by major divisions of the Lutheran Church in America and the American Lutheran Church. Again, it was an "opinion changing" experience. One young man described a pattern of one-night stands that made the group feel ill at ease. His boast about many sexual partners was met with a strong sense of rejection for that way of life. But he was the exception. Others in the group told of long-term relationships and commitment to only one other person. And, again, listeners had to be impressed at the strong Christian conviction of several gay and lesbian persons who served as resources for the conference.

Events like these helped both of us to begin to take some cautious steps across the spectrum. We could no longer accept the notion that homosexuality was a chosen orientation; for many people we had met we could not conceive of a change in their sexual orientation.

Though we had changed in our thinking about some aspects of the issue, both of us remained convinced that gays and lesbians should not be involved in an intimate relationship with a person of the same gender. We embraced the often-quoted phrase: "Love the sinner, but hate the sin." We were saying to people in the gay community, "I'm sorry you are gay, and I wish it were otherwise. I understand that you must have strong sexual feelings toward some persons of the same sex, but just as there are many heterosexual persons who, for whatever reason, are not involved in an intimate sexual relationship, so it must be for you."

Though Christians in the gay community were disappointed with our stance, they realized that both of us had open minds and were willing to keep talking to them. Over time more and more of them came out to us and shared both their disappointment with the church as well as their love for Christ and the church. By the mid-1980s, we knew many homosexual people, including several pastors and many gay and lesbian children of Lutheran pastors. Many were in long-term relationships. We found them to be as devoted to each other as any of our straight, married friends.

By the early 1990s, we found that we had moved clear across the spectrum. By then we were convinced that homosexuality is not a choice but a discovery, that gay and lesbian persons should be afforded full civil rights, and that their relationships of trust and fidelity should be affirmed. We saw that sexual orientation for gay and lesbian persons, like that of heterosexuals, is not just the physical magnetism of sexual attraction, but is also an orientation of affection, love, and yearning to be loved. We came to understand that it involves not only the urges of the body but the longings of heart, mind, and spirit for life-giving companionship and lifelong friendship.

Out of all these experiences we have come to a place where we affirm life-giving sexual fulfillment for gays and lesbians and welcome the creation of responsible, committed same-sex relationships that are the moral and emotional equivalent of marriage. We encourage those in such relationships to live together with the same kind of mutual love, mutual respect, mutual openness, and mutual faithfulness that we have envisioned for heterosexual marriage.

THREE CRITICAL QUESTIONS

We believe that there are three questions at the heart of all these issues that can be asked of heterosexual and homosexual persons:

Is Sexual Orientation a Choice for Heterosexual Persons?

We find it important to begin by asking this question of ourselves and other straight people. Did we choose? No. Like other heterosexuals, neither of us can recall a time when we decided to be straight. As we moved into puberty, we found girls to be marvelously attractive. Like all heterosexual boys, we began to fantasize about some of the most attractive girls we knew. As young Christians, we also began to pray that God would one day make it clear who the women were with whom we would share our lives—all of our lives.

No, it had not been a choice. It just was.

Can Heterosexuals Change Their Orientation?

The very idea is unthinkable to both of us as straight persons. How could we ever change? It would be impossible. Even if we allowed someone to make a concerted effort to change us, it would fail. Like all straight people, we find that sexual orientation is integral to who we are as human beings.

No, we could never change. This is who we are.

How Should Heterosexuals Live?

For straight people the church has had a clear answer. Those who have not committed themselves to another person in marriage should refrain from an intimate genital sexual relationship. Those who marry should be faithful to their spouse.

We know that sexual practice, even among Christians, is often far from this standard. We indicated earlier, pastors who ask find that a strong majority of couples have premarital sex. We also know that though the percentage is lower than in society in general, church members stray at times from their promises of fidelity.

How should we live as heterosexuals? We affirm the church's traditional stance, though it is sometimes broken: Genital intimacy belongs in the setting of strong, faithful, lifelong commitment to one other person.

Having asked these questions of those of us who are straight, we may be ready to ask these queries about gay and lesbian persons.

Is Sexual Orientation a Choice for Homosexual Persons?

When we raise this question with persons who have a definite homosexual orientation they are as incredulous as we are when asked if we chose to be heterosexual. Most of them say that they first became aware of their sexual inclination when they were very young. They realized that they were different from their friends whenever the subject of attraction to the opposite sex came up.

No, it is no more a choice for them than it is for heterosexuals.

Can Homosexuals Change Their Orientation?

Given the kind of world we live in, where there is gay-bashing and constant affirmation of straight relationships, it's not surprising that some homosexual persons seek ways to change. But again and again, and often after years of struggle and pain and considerable financial expense, they usually come to a settled acceptance of themselves as homosexual.

No, change is not possible for one who has known only attraction to others of the same gender.

How Should Homosexuals Live?

There are many people who have moved on the attitude spectrum. They believe that homosexuality is not a choice. They affirm that it is difficult, if not impossible, to change. But then they stop where we once were. They believe that gays and lesbians must refrain from intimate relationships.

Both of us have moved beyond that stage in our own thinking. If we accept the notion that homosexual persons are genuinely sexual beings with strong desires to share in an intimate relationship, then it seems unconscionable to deny them the privilege of such life-giving companionship. We would stress, however, that the standards for such relationships should be the same as those we expect of heterosexuals. That is to say, it should be a long-term commitment of love, trust, and fidelity.

We are keenly and sadly aware of the fact that some homosexual persons engage in sex with multiple partners. We understand, of course, that part of the blame for this destructive way of living rests with the larger culture that will not affirm same-sex relationships. We do not believe, however, that this can be used as an excuse for a way of life that is dangerous to their physical, mental, and spiritual well being. Life-giving sexual relationships are not death-dealing. Sexual encounters that may cause sickness and death, whether between heterosexual or homosexual partners, are not acts of love.

We believe that all intimate sexual relationships can only have meaning when they are carried on in the context of a deep commitment of one person to another—a commitment that has the blessing of the community and that is, as with heterosexual relationships, for a lifetime.

In his explanation of the commandment "You shall not commit adultery," Luther suggests in a very positive way that "we are to fear and love God so that in matters of sex our words and conduct are pure and honorable." We believe that same high standard should be the guide for homosexual relationships.

There are those who believe that genital experimentation may be a necessary part of the process of gays and lesbians coming to full discovery of their sexual orientation. We fear that such experimenting, like heterosexual testing of sexual compatibility by having relations prior to a committed relationship, would be like testing a parachute by jumping out of a fifth-story window. Without sufficient height, a parachute cannot be tested. Without sufficient depth, a sexual relationship cannot be tested.

SHALL WE BLESS THEM?

Should same-sex relationships be blessed? Several states now recognize same-sex partnerships, and at least one has affirmed "civil unions" with benefits comparable to those of marriage. When such couples appear at our church doors, it is obvious that we must deal with them. Those of us who believe that committed Christian same-sex relationships should be affirmed now seek ways for the church, in some way, to bless them.

Christians who have moved this far in their affirmation of gay and lesbian relationships have differing opinions concerning how to do so. Some pastors now share prayers of blessing with same-sex couples in confidential counseling sessions. Others conduct home blessing services that include prayers for the occupants and not only the dwelling.

There are some congregations where ministry to and with gay and lesbian persons has become so much a part of their identity that public blessing of relationships has not been a problem for either the parish, neighboring congregations, or the denomination. Though some make a strong case for using traditional language, we favor avoiding words like *marriage, wedding,* and *holy matrimony.* These terms are so deeply associated with heterosexual marriage that we believe it only sets back the cause by using them. Possibly phrases such as "blessing of a relationship" or "blessed union" or "holy union" could be used. Whatever the case, we would challenge all of us to think of other words and phrases to describe committed Christian gay and lesbian unions. When doing so, however, we must be ready to support people in these relationships and to see that they are accorded the same rights and privileges as straight couples in church and in society. If the pastor cannot perform such a ceremony, a layperson could do so with a pastor present (Wall, 739).

Before a public service of blessing is conducted in the church building, it is wise to inform and secure the support of the congregational council. If there is more opposition than support, it is usually better to have a private service of blessing in another place and to work for the day when the congregation recognizes such blessings as a proper part of the parish's caring ministry with some of God's too often despised and rejected children.

We hope that bishops, pastors, and members of other congregations will have the patience, grace, and understanding to allow this to happen in certain places in the church. The church is strong. It can tolerate, and even affirm, a variety of practice. This may be the door through which the church can enter into a new and dynamic ministry in an area where we have failed until now.

SOME BASIC QUESTIONS

It's important to ask ourselves some fundamental questions: Can we go on pretending that these relationships do not exist? Can we go on denying the ministry of grace to those who are in committed, faithful relationships? Can we exclude these confessing Christians from full participation in the life of the church? Can we call them to the same high standards and ideals of heterosexual marriage unless we affirm homosexual partnerships and work to make them stronger?

Ordain Qualified Homosexuals in Committed Relationships?

Churches have always ordained homosexual persons. Most of the time, of course, churches did not know they were doing it. When openly gay and lesbian persons and their supporters have requested ordination, they have been met with varied responses. Most churches have denied them this privilege. Some denominations have approved their ordination so long as they refrain from a same-sex relationship. A few denominations have approved the ordination of homosexual persons in long-term relationships of faithfulness.

In 1988, when some chose to test the Evangelical Lutheran Church in America (ELCA) on this issue early in its new life, that church, through its synod bishops, denied ordination to those in same-sex relationships. The bishops stated that only those gay and lesbian people who refrained from such relationships could be ordained.

Both of us were bishops at that time—one the presiding bishop of the church and the other a synod bishop. Like the majority of our colleagues, we believed that the ordination of homosexuals who would not commit themselves to celibacy would divide our young and fragile church. But we are now convinced that there has been a shift in attitudes in the church over these past years. Many have studied the issue thoroughly and have changed their minds about the nature of homosexuality. We are guardedly hopeful that our church may be at the place where it can accept and even welcome some change in this area of its life.

To put it succinctly: We believe that openly gay and lesbian persons should be ordained by the same standards as straight persons. Just as we require single, straight people seeking ordination to refrain from sexual activity, so can we expect abstinence from homosexuals who are not in committed relationships. Homosexual persons who have a partner should be expected to live in a commitment of lifelong devotion to that person, just as we expect of heterosexual persons who are married.

In the context of grace we in the ELCA, like fellow Christians in most denominations, have remained united in spite of significant differences about many complex and controversial issues, including abortion, capital punishment, war, divorce and remarriage, ecumenical relationships, infant communion, styles of worship, and many more. We pray and work for a church that is so solidly centered and united in Jesus Christ that we can work and witness together in spite of significant differences, even those concerning human sexuality.

How, Then, Can Change Come About?

Change will likely come gradually and in informal ways, as is already happening in some places. When a proposal calling for a moratorium on denial of ordination came before a national assembly of the Evangelical Lutheran Church in America in 1999, it failed by a wide margin—as it has with many other churches that have brought it to a vote at a convention. So we must ask, "Is our church at the point where we are strong enough and secure enough to welcome differences from place to place? Can we permit some congregations that are deeply committed to ministry to and with gay and lesbian people to call pastors who are in long-term commitments of fidelity to persons of the same gender? Are there some synod bishops who affirm such relationships and serve in areas where congregations can allow for this kind of diversity? Will other bishops and synods allow for such variety?"

Before we reject this idea out of hand, let us review the history of how churches have changed their practice in other areas where there was much contention at one time. Slavery is one such area. For hundreds of years, churches supported slavery, often with citations from the Bible. In time, that changed. Christians came to believe that it was wrong for one person to own another. Over a period of time, more and more churches came to believe that they must change their policy. But few did it by formal action. More often than not it happened because members of congregations changed their attitudes and then their actions. As more time passed, church bodies caught up with them and adopted practices giving equal status to all members.

Divorce is another example. When we were ordained into the Lutheran ministry in the late 1950s, no pastor—no matter what the circumstance—could remain in the ministry following a divorce. Over time this, too, changed. Here and there bishops decided that this issue needed to be handled pastorally on a case-by-case basis. Today there are many divorced and remarried pastors who are serving effectively in the ELCA and many other denominations. The ELCA and its predecessor church bodies never acted in an official way on the matter of clergy divorce and remarriage. In the course of time each situation was dealt with pastorally and the practice of automatically excluding such pastors was quietly dropped.

WHAT DOES THE BIBLE SAY?

We saved this question until last because we believe it is easier to understand the role of the Bible if we have first set out the issues.

Before we get involved with specific texts, however, it's important to ask ourselves a few preparatory questions: What is the fundamental purpose of the Bible? Why was it written? What is at its heart? As Lutheran pastors and former bishops, we have always believed and taught that the basic purpose of the Bible is to lead us to a living faith and trust in Jesus Christ as our Savior. When we use the phrase "the Word of God" it means, first and foremost, Jesus Christ. He is the Word who was in the beginning and was with God. He became flesh and lived among us, full of grace and truth (John 1:1, 14). Everything we do in the church should be pointed toward that purpose—that all might know the truth concerning Jesus (Luke 1:4).

But what about the Bible as a guide for living? Can't we go to the Bible and find an infallible resource that will help us to understand exactly how we should think about all the complex issues of life and that will tell us how to live in a very complicated world?

We affirm the Bible as our basic guide for faith and life. There is no better source of understanding that concerns how we should live. We are profoundly grateful for all the good things we see around us that are the result of work done by people inspired by the teachings of the Bible. Why do people give to world hunger programs, care for the sick and the aged, reach out to troubled youth, develop programs to protect and nurture children? While many do these things without reference to the Bible, we know that others have been called to service by some direct word of Scripture.

But now come the hard questions: What do we do with those parts of the Bible that mandate customs for certain social situations that no longer exist? We surely don't want to set aside the Ten Commandments. But what about all those dietary and ceremonial laws in the Old Testament, for example, that no longer apply to us today?

It soon becomes clear that though the Bible is indeed a wonderful guide for living, it does not anticipate every conceivable situation, nor does it give us easy answers to new and complex questions that confront us almost every day.

What about the issue of homosexuality? Entire volumes have been written about this question alone. Before we reflect on some of the texts, we believe there are some things that can be said very succinctly: We have asserted throughout this volume that the Bible affirms us as sexual beings. Sex is more than a way to propagate the human family. It is also a gift to be shared and enjoyed. We believe that the Bible speaks clearly and forcefully against many forms of sexual immorality—heterosexual and homosexual.

We acknowledge that there are no passages in the Bible that specifically affirm homosexual relationships. Any attempt to find such texts results in reading into the Bible more than what is there. At the same time, we agree with biblical scholars who point out that the texts that speak negatively about homosexual immorality are often difficult to translate and are subject to differing interpretations.

Biblical References to Homosexuality

We believe that the story of Sodom and Gomorrah in Genesis 19 is about homosexual immorality. But it is *also* about heterosexual immorality and inhospitality—as is pointed out in subsequent references. One can hardly argue from this text that both heterosexual and homosexual relationships are therefore always immoral. All one can say is that the kinds of abusive immorality described at Sodom and Gomorrah are to be condemned. We believe that this story is not relevant to our current discussion regarding long-term relationships of commitment, love, and trust between consenting partners of the same gender.

The condemnation of homosexual relationships in Leviticus 18:22 seems conclusive: "You shall not lie with a male as with a woman; it is an abomination." But how does one distinguish this law from others in that same moral code that we believe were for that time only? A man and woman caught in an extramarital affair, for example, were to be stoned to death, as was a rebellious child (Lev. 20:10). Who would think of doing this today?

We conclude that the most we can say is that these laws may have been important for the preservation of the community of Israel in its infancy. But should they be applied today without reference to our changed situation? We think not.

As for the passages in Romans 1, 1 Corinthians 6, and Jude, New Testament scholars are deeply divided in their interpretations. Some insist that they mean exactly what they seem to say, namely that all homosexual relationships are wrong. We side with those who believe that Paul's major concern is with injustice and that the list of vices makes that apparent. Among those vices are certain sexual sins, such as the domination by one person of another. In addition, we believe that Paul has in mind relationships between men and boys—relationships we all would condemn. In those days some non-Christian cults practiced homosexual activity. Some scholars believe that Paul is warning against the danger of idolatry resulting from consorting with non-Christian priests and priestesses. If these conclusions are correct, the realities of homosexual orientation and same-sex relationships of faithfulness and trust between consenting adults are never addressed anywhere in the Bible.

But suppose we're wrong. Suppose Paul had in mind same-sex adult relationships of commitment. Are we necessarily bound by his word as the last word? We do well to note that there were many practices that Paul affirmed—especially regarding the role of women in the church—that do not bind us today. What, for example, do we do with Paul's word to the church at Corinth that "the wife should not separate from her husband (but if she does separate, let her remain unmarried or else be reconciled to her husband), and . . . the husband should not divorce his wife" (1 Cor. 7:10-11)? Few of us would want to see these rules enforced today.

Paul most certainly did not know what we know today about the nature of homosexuality. Many believe that in the context of the gospel of grace, Jesus (who said nothing about this issue) would affirm those who agree to live in a responsible and faithful same-sex union. None of us, of course, knows for certain what Jesus would say or do. But we are driven back to our original question about the purpose of the Bible—that we be led to faith and trust in Jesus as Savior. In that context we can wrestle together with these difficult questions.

Our own conclusion is that there are no specific references in the New Testament to the question that most concerns us—the long-term commitment of love and trust between consenting persons of the same gender.

It is also important to underscore the fact that Christians do not derive their ethical and social teachings from the Bible alone. We believe that all truth is God's truth and that wisdom received from the natural and social sciences is a vital element in our ethical decision making. Our understanding of human sexuality, especially of sexual orientation, has been greatly enhanced by the scientific discoveries of the past century. We now have information and insights that were unknown and, therefore, never considered in biblical times. To ignore, to deny, these realities is, we believe, a betrayal of God's gifts of knowledge and reason.

SIGNS OF HOPE

Given the fractured nature of the discussion of this subject in most of our churches, we cannot expect resolution in the near future. That there has been movement in the direction of greater understanding of homosexuality is encouraging. Now it is clear that the issue is not just for large metropolitan areas like New York, Chicago, and San Francisco. Even our most rural communities have become painfully aware that they must wrestle with it as well.

The growing number of gay and lesbian Christians who have had the courage to be more open about their sexuality has probably been the most significant factor in bringing change. There are now millions of families who know someone in their immediate or extended circle who is gay or lesbian. When we know one of these people firsthand, it changes the dynamics of the discussion. Now we are often speaking about someone we love and respect. Now we are drawn into the question of rights and privileges for someone we know to be a whole person, a person who deserves the same treatment in church and society that we accord ourselves.

But change comes ever so slowly in those areas where there has been such a long tradition of strong difference of opinion. As we have pointed out, it took our nation—in spite of its high democratic ideals—more than a century and a half to begin to give equal rights to African Americans and others. And even today the marks of prejudice and hate are still apparent in our communities.

The same is true for the church. Regardless of the difficulties we have cited regarding biblical interpretation, we believe the heart of the gospel calls for justice for all God's children. In spite of our ideals, the church remains segregated in most places and often lags far behind other entities in calling for justice.

THE MIRACLE OF DIALOGUE

Although the goal may seem distant, the calling of the church is to keep open the doors of dialogue. We need to practice not only "the art of the possible" but also "the art of making possible tomorrow what seems impossible today." When we see injustice against gay and lesbian people, we are obliged to speak up. When we have an opportunity to advance legislation that will redress long-standing wrongs, we must work for it.

Above all, we must continue to discuss these issues in our churches. We believe, as stated in the introduction to this book, "that we are dealing with not only sex but issues of truth and justice and, above all, the life fulfillment of human beings." Many mainline denominations have spent a great deal of energy on this question in the past twenty years. We may be tempted to push it aside and gain a bit of respite. That would be a mistake. Our gay and lesbian sisters and brothers in Christ have been more patient than we have a right to expect. Passage of resolutions of support for them at church conventions must be accompanied by concrete affirmation of justice as well as love and goodwill in our local congregations. To genuinely welcome gays and lesbians into full participation in our churches, we must not only invite them to sing in our choirs, be our organists, read the lessons, and teach our children; we must also seek ways of affirming their sexual fulfillment in loving, lifelong, committed relationships and to explore creative ways to help those who are called and qualified on all other grounds to enter the pastoral ministry of our churches. We are convinced that there are gay and lesbian persons in faithful relationships that have a call from God to be pastors. By what authority can we deny them their calling to Christian ministry?

When Christians of goodwill are open to dialogue and to new understandings of God's will, when they are respectful of contrary opinions, when they search together for greater understanding of the meaning of God's love in Christ—when these things happen, there is healing and there is hope.

QUESTIONS & ANSWERS

Q: I am one of your colleagues in ministry. I have never been married, but was once engaged to a wonderful woman for whom I cared deeply and who was one of the best friends I have ever known. I looked forward to spending my life with her but discovered when we parked in the moonlight that I never became sexually aroused or felt any sexual attraction toward her. At the same time, I had to confess, though always only to myself, that I did experience sexual attraction toward some men. This was, for me, a horrifying discovery. I hoped that I would experience at least some sexual attraction in my relationship with my fiancée, but it never happened. I finally decided, even while we were planning for our wedding, that I had to break our engagement and end our relationship. It was one of the most painful things I have ever experienced, and it was especially difficult because I didn't dare tell her the real reason for my doing so.

Nor have I dared share this secret with others. I have had a meaningful ministry, and I have many good friends, but I have always been ashamed of who I am, and only in recent years have I begun to believe that these feelings of shame are terribly mistaken. Now that I am near retirement I have been brave enough to come out to a few close friends who have graciously accepted me as I am, but oh how I wish that might have happened earlier. All these years I have carried the burden of what seemed to me a shameful secret, and although I've always been sociable and outgoing, at heart I've been sad and lonely all my life.

I've also begun to realize that I have been angry with God and with the church. Angry with God for making me the way I am, angry with the church for teaching me that I am a shameful abomination. Now as I have finally begun to experience some acceptance and affirmation, I have also begun to believe that maybe God didn't make a terrible mistake when he created me the way I am and that God might even be angry with the church for teaching me to despise myself.

I make this confession in the hope that it will help you understand people like me and also to encourage you to do what you can to help the church be more understanding and affirming of gay and lesbian people and especially of those who are, or would like to be, pastors in the church. At long last I dare to believe that God loves and affirms us, and I long for the day when the church will also do so.

A: Thank you for sharing your story. You have helped us to understand and to feel some of your grief and pain. We are sorry that your experience of acceptance and affirmation didn't come much earlier. We ask your forgiveness for all we have done that has added to your burden and for all we have failed to do to increase understanding and affirmation of gay and lesbian people.

Perhaps more than anything else it was conversations with courageous people like you beginning many years ago that compelled us to confront our own misunderstandings of homosexuality. Your letter convicts and challenges us to repent of our past failures, and we now pray for love, wisdom, and courage to respond in ways that will make a difference in both church and in society.

Thank you for your moving testimony. God bless you always.

Q: My partner and I have known each other for seven years. We were good friends before we became lovers. Before beginning to live together three years ago, we shared promises of love and commitment to each other and intend our relationship to be lifelong.

We are active in our church. Both of us sing in the choir and have volunteered to help with the church school and other activities. We believe that God has given us as a gift to each other, and thank God every day for our life together. We have visited several times with our pastor and have asked if he would perform a service of blessing of our relationship. He has prayed with us in his office and has asked God to bless us in our life together, but has also said that he doesn't think that it would be right for him to conduct a public service of blessing. He thinks that it would cause conflict in the church and get him in trouble with his denomination. We have shared our desire for blessing with several good friends in the congregation and have always felt welcomed and affirmed by everyone in the parish. We don't want to cause trouble for our church or our pastor. What do you think we should do?

A: On the basis of what you have shared with us, we affirm your desire to have a service of blessing and also empathize with your pastor's reluctance to perform it.

Because your pastor has personally affirmed and privately prayed for God's blessing on your life together, we wonder if he would be open to conducting a service of home blessing at your place of residence to which close friends and family could be invited and which would invoke God's blessing, not only on the place, but also upon the people who live there. This event need not be secret, nor would it need to be announced in the church bulletin. It would be a service for you and invited family and friends. For the pastor it would be an act of personal, pastoral care. And like many such acts, it is essentially a private event involving only the pastor and the participants.

If your pastor is not open to such a service, we encourage you to respect his judgment. He may know of someone who would be willing to conduct a service of blessing (remember that this could be a layperson). You may even wish to invite him to attend such a service as a guest or to show his support by attending the reception afterward. If he does not know of anyone to whom to refer you, we suggest that you visit with people in church-related gay/lesbian support groups. They will be able to tell you of congregations, pastors, and laypersons that conduct same-sex services of commitment and blessing. If you need help in finding such organizations, several are listed in the resources at the end of this book.

Thanks again for sharing your concerns. May grace abound to sustain and strengthen you in your life together. God bless you always.

Q: I have heard and read some of the things you have said about welcoming homosexuals and even blessing their relationships and finding ways of getting them into the pastoral ministry of the church and I want you to know that I think you are terribly mistaken and are leading the church astray. You must know that the Bible declares homosexuality to be an abomination.

I know that God loves sinners and that we are to love them, too. I also believe that we are to hate sin and not to condone it. Therefore, I encourage you to get back to the Bible and to teach only biblical truths.

A: We, too, affirm biblical truth. But we don't believe that the Bible says anything about homosexuality as we understand it today. The Bible condemns certain types of sexual practices such as homosexual rape and the pagan practice of men using boys for sexual purposes. It says nothing about homosexual orientation, which wasn't scientifically discovered and analyzed until hundreds of years after the Bible was written, or about faithful, committed relationships between persons of the same sex.

We believe that it is as unfair to conclude from the Bible's condemnation of certain sinful homosexual practices that all homosexual activity is sinful as it would be to conclude from a book describing heterosexual rape and child molestation that all heterosexual activity is sinful. To use the Bible to condemn homosexual persons and committed faithful same-sex relationships is, we believe, to bear false witness against the Bible.

We also want to assure you that we are against all sin whether it is homosexual, heterosexual, or nonsexual. We understand sin in light of Christ-centered texts such as this passage from the apostle Paul:

> Owe no one anything, except to love one another; for the one who loves another has fulfilled the law. The commandments, "You shall not commit adultery; you shall not murder; you shall not steal; you shall not covet"; and any other commandment, are summed up in this word, "Love your neighbor as yourself." Love does no wrong to a neighbor; therefore, love is the fulfilling of the law. (Rom. 13:8-10)

We understand the written word of Scripture in light of Jesus who is the living Word. Christ, who is Lord of all, is also Lord of the Bible. Apart from such Christ-centered interpretation, the Bible has been, and still can be, used to affirm slavery, polygamy, and concubinage. You challenge us to get back to the Bible. We trust you are not encouraging us to use that kind of biblical interpretation. There are significant differences among biblical scholars concerning these matters. If you are serious about such study, we encourage you to read recent books published by Augsburg Fortress: *Pastoral Care of Gays, Lesbians, and Their Families* by David K. Switzer; *Homoeroticism in the Biblical World: A Historical Perspective* by Martti Nissinen; *Homosexuality and Christian Faith* edited by Walter Wink; and the chapter on homosexuality in Paul Jersild's book *Spirit Ethics: Scripture and the Moral Life.* We also encourage you to read *Heterosexism: An Ethical Challenge* by Patricia Jung and Ralph Smith who were formerly professors at Wartburg Theological Seminary. For the moving personal testimony of an evangelical Christian, read Mel White's *Stranger at the Gate.*

We don't claim to have all the answers concerning complex and controversial issues of human sexuality, but we have studied Scripture carefully and believe the positions we have taken are affirmed by responsible biblical scholarship.

Q: Although I hate to make this confession, I am so tormented by anxiety that I have to share it with someone. I recently attended an X-rated movie theater that presented a number of short and exceedingly explicit portrayals of sexual encounters. Several were between men and women, one involved several men, and another pictured two women who were sexually involved with each other. Of all that sexual activity the one that was by far the most arousing to me involved the two women, and that makes me wonder if I'm gay.

Having confessed my attendance at that movie, I should probably also confess that I have never been sexually involved with anyone but I am dating a wonderful woman and plan to ask her to marry me. But now I am in a panic. What if I'm gay? If so, wouldn't it be a terrible mistake for me to marry anybody? Please help me understand this whole business of "sexual orientation."

A: We consulted with a psychiatrist concerning your experience and his comments confirmed our conviction that it is exceedingly unlikely that you are gay. In watching a movie, sexual or otherwise, we tend to identify with the characters and to feel emotions of fear, sadness, joy, or whatever they are experiencing. You apparently identified with one or both of those lesbian lovers, imagined yourself being involved in what they were doing, and discovered that you were strongly sexually aroused. If you were a woman, that might reveal lesbian leanings, but since you are a man we think that it confirms the fact that you are heterosexual, that is, sexually attracted to persons of the opposite sex.

What turns people on sexually is an extremely complex, highly personal matter. Few, if any, of us are purely, 100 percent heterosexual or homosexual. Persons who are strongly heterosexual certainly aren't sexually attracted to every person of the other sex, nor are strongly homosexual persons sexually attracted to every person of the same sex. Even persons with such clear and strong sexual orientation may be surprised to discover themselves to have at least mild sexual attraction to some people of the same or opposite sex. Those who discover themselves to have strong affectional and sexual attraction to persons of both sexes are described as being "bisexual" in their orientation. Our understanding is that sexual orientation is discovered rather than chosen, and that stories of people who have "changed" from gay to straight usually describe the experience of persons who are at least somewhat bisexual and who have now found someone of the opposite sex with the combination of qualities they personally find sexually attractive.

There are also those who have been so abused by persons of the other sex, perhaps a parent or sibling, relative or other significant adult, that they can no longer trust or respect anyone of that gender. Women who hate men and men who despise women may have great difficulty relating to persons of the other sex, but that does not mean that they are lesbian or gay. If their feelings are healed through prayer, learning, and therapy, they may be able to enter meaningful heterosexual relationships, but this does not indicate a change in their sexual orientation.

To us you seem to be strongly heterosexual, but if you are still anxious concerning your personal sexual orientation, we encourage you to visit with a psychiatrist or even to seek a personal evaluation of your orientation. A program at the University of Minnesota offers such a service. We assume that it is available elsewhere. If you desire such an evaluation, a pastor or counselor in your area should be able to secure information and make a referral.

Q: I am a junior in high school and have a problem I don't dare talk to anybody about. I don't even like to think about it, but I can't go on like this, and hope that it is safe for me to share it with you.

For a long time I have felt that I am different from other guys. Most of them seem to spend half their lives thinking about girls. They talk about making out and get all excited over the pictures in *Playboy* magazine, which don't seem very sexy to me. I have done some dating and took a girl to the prom, but I have never felt like making out with any of them.

I've developed a very close friendship with one of the guys in our class. We have never done anything sexual or even talked about it, but I have sexual thoughts about him and get very jealous when he spends a lot of time with other people and seems to ignore me. I sometimes even daydream about our doing sexual things together.

All of this really scares me and makes me wonder if I am a homosexual. I have read everything I can find on the subject and the more I read, the more scared I get. I am active in sports and don't think that I look or talk like a gay person, but I feel really uncomfortable when I hear guys making jokes about "homos." Do you think I'm gay? If so, what can I do to get over it? I hope you can help me. I sure need it.

A: Thank you for trusting us with your concerns. On the basis of what you have shared with us, we think it is possible, perhaps even probable, that you are a person of homosexual orientation. If that is true, it means that you are one of the many people in the world who discover themselves to be sexually attracted primarily to persons of the same sex.

It is difficult to know for sure whether a person of your age is homosexual or heterosexual. Many adolescents develop strong attachments with peers of the same sex, but this does not mean that they are all homosexual. The dynamics of sexual attraction are extremely complex. A lot of people are, to some extent, bisexual, that is, they experience sexual attraction to some people of both the same and the opposite sex. We think that it is important for you to find a competent person with whom to share your concerns honestly and from whom you can learn more about who you are and about sexual orientation. Perhaps your school counselor, a favorite teacher, your pastor, or medical doctor could be that person. If you live near a major university that has a program in human sexuality, they could be of help to you.

Whatever you do, we believe it is wise for you to refrain from sexual activity with your friend and think it will be best if you don't tell him of your feelings toward him. We also discourage you from getting sexually involved with a girl in an attempt to prove that you are not homosexual. That kind of test doesn't prove anything.

Whatever your sexual orientation, remember that it is a gift from God. Sexual orientation seems to be determined quite early in life by factors we don't fully understand. It is not chosen but discovered, and there doesn't seem to be anything we can do to significantly change it. You are now in the process of making that discovery, and we encourage you to keep on doing your best in high school, being involved in sports, and having lots of friendships with both guys and girls. We believe that as time goes on, your orientation will become more clear to you and that your ongoing conversations with a competent counselor will also be helpful. If it turns out that you are gay, remember you are no less capable of living a good and joyful life than a straight person is. There is increasing understanding and acceptance of gay and lesbian people in both the church and society. In the grace of God many homosexual Christians have discovered, as they like to say, that "gay is good" and that they can find much joy and fulfillment in life. Jesus came to give you life in fullness (see John 10:10). God loves you and will love you forever. Rest in that love.

Q: I am a seminary student who has done well in my studies and who feels deeply called to pastoral ministry. I am also a lesbian and am in a committed and faithful relationship. We had a service of blessing of our relationship in our congregation, so our life together is not a secret.

My denomination willingly ordains gay and lesbian people who, in effect, take a vow of chastity, but it does not ordain those who are in a relationship. Following my graduation from seminary I would like to serve as a pastor of a congregation, but present rules prevent me from doing so. Therefore, my only hope of serving as a pastor in this church is either for the rules to change or for a congregation to break the rules and to call and ordain me on its own. I could try to change denominations, but I love my church and don't want to leave. Do you see any hope of my becoming a pastor? What do you think I should do?

A: From what we know of your denomination, it's unlikely the present policy will soon be changed. At the same time, we hope that practices related to the enforcement of the policy will soon become more pastoral and less rigid.

We wish, for example, that your denomination would find a way to begin to make exceptions for persons like you. There is a wise old saying that "exceptions prove the rule." Gracious wisdom is pastoral, not legalistic. We believe that affirmation of exceptions to the present rule, for the sake of ministry in specific settings, would be an expression of such gracious wisdom.

In other words, the change would not be in policy but in polity, that is, in the procedures dealing with the situation. If procedures were modified, your call could be dealt with locally and pastorally. If your denomination did not wish to include you on the roster of ordained clergy, they could still recognize that you are an ordained pastor serving that congregation. They could even issue an ecclesiastical reprimand but wouldn't need to be so severe as to expel the parish from the church.

If neither policy nor polity is modified, you could serve a congregation in a lay pastoral ministry position doing almost everything that is done by ordained pastors, or you could be called and ordained by a congregation acting with conscientious ecclesiastical disobedience, if there is a willing parish. This might cause a major disruption or, depending upon the pastoral wisdom of the bishop and other church leaders, it might be dealt with in ways that would model new procedures helpful to the church at large. We have lived long enough to know that what happens in the church depends not only upon the letter of ecclesiastical regulations but also upon the wisdom and compassion of those who administer them. We pray that the leaders of your denomination will have an abundance of wisdom, compassion, and courage in dealing with your situation and that, for the sake of the ministry of the church as well as the fulfillment of your call, you will be able to be ordained. May grace abound for the continued fulfillment of your life and ministry.

Q: My husband and I have a problem that is causing tension between us. Our twenty-seven-year-old son recently told us that he is gay and is now living with his "friend." This was a terrible shock to both of us. We have three other children who seem to be happily married, and we can't understand why this has happened to us. We treated all our children the same and wonder how we went wrong?

I have continued to keep in touch with our son, but my husband is so hurt and angry that he refuses to have anything to do with him. He has even threatened to write him out of our will. He has told me to stop calling our son and would be outraged if he knew that I once had lunch with him and his partner, who seems like a fine young man. I don't want to offend or lie to my husband, but I also don't want to cut off contact with our son. I feel caught between a rock and a hard place. What do you think I should do?

A: We empathize with your difficult situation and hope that you will be able to have a good relationship with both your husband and your son.

Our first response is to share a little poem by Dr. Gerhard Frost, whose daughter Ruth, ordained by a local Lutheran congregation, has been in a committed relationship with another woman pastor for a number of years. We wonder if he had them in mind when he wrote these lines:

When your options are either
to revise your beliefs
or to reject a person,
look again.

Any formula for living
that is too cramped
for the human situation
cries for rethinking.

Hard-cover catechisms
are a contradiction
to our loose-leaf lives.

We also recall someone saying years ago that "we parents need to hold our children tightly with an open hand."

More specifically, we don't know why some people discover themselves to be homosexual and their siblings heterosexual, but we are convinced that a person's sexual orientation is not the result of either good or bad parenting. We therefore encourage you to be neither proud nor guilty over your children's sexual orientation.

Since so many sons and daughters are now finding the honesty and courage to reveal their same-sex orientation to their parents, there must be thousands of families who are sharing an experience similar to yours.

There is an organization called PFLAG (see resource list at the end of the book) that provides support for parents, family, and friends of lesbians and gays. We hope that you will find a group near you and get acquainted with people who know firsthand what you are going through. We encourage your husband to go with you. If he refuses, go by yourself. You will almost certainly meet several people who understand your husband's feelings and will be open to visiting with him. They may be able to help bring your family together again.

Q: I am happily married and have a satisfying sexual relationship with my husband, but I must also confess something that I have never shared with anyone. I also have feelings of sexual attraction toward some women. Until the last few years I don't think that I have ever admitted this, even to myself. In high school and college I had several close girlfriends toward whom I had such feelings, and there are now times when I daydream about sexual involvement with my best friend.

I have never acted on these feelings and have never said a word to anyone about them. Nor do I think that I have ever behaved in ways that would reveal them, or that I would ever do so.

Do you think that such thoughts and feelings are sinful? What can I do to get rid of them?

A: Our initial reaction is to say, "Welcome to the human race." If everyone were honest and open, you would discover that there are a lot of people who have similar thoughts and feelings. We wish that everyone were as responsible in dealing with them as you are.

A half-century ago Alfred Kinsey and others observed that there is a spectrum of sexual attraction ranging from nearly exclusive attraction to persons of the opposite sex to nearly exclusive attraction to persons of the same sex, and that there are lots of degrees of difference in between. Those who are around the middle of the spectrum are often described as being "bisexual," that is, they experience significant sexual and affectional attraction to persons of both sexes. We would never attempt to classify anyone on the basis of a few brief comments, but we believe it is possible that you have what might be called bisexual capacities. This is not bad. People do not choose their sexual orientation; they discover it in the sexual awakening of adolescence and young adulthood. We believe that it is wise for us to receive and regard that orientation, whatever it may be, as the good gift of a loving God and then to pray for the wisdom and courage to live with it responsibly.

We don't think that there is anything that you can do to change your thoughts and feelings. Martin Luther liked to say that we can't keep the birds from flying over our heads, but we can keep them from making nests in our hair. It sounds as if that is exactly how you have been living, and we commend you.

You are in a committed relationship with your husband and you indicate that you are happy, experience sexual satisfaction in your marriage, and have no intention of acting on your feelings of same-sex attraction. Unlike strongly oriented heterosexuals and homosexuals, bisexuals have a choice—not concerning their orientation but concerning whether to be involved in a heterosexual or homosexual relationship. We affirm faithfulness to one other person for all people. You have made the choice of a committed heterosexual marriage. We believe that your greatest life fulfillment lies in being faithful to that commitment.

If your same-sex attraction were so strong and your other-sex attraction so weak that a heterosexual marriage would be impossible for you, we would have a different response; on the basis of what you have shared with us, however, we wish you and your husband continued joy in your life together, and we encourage you to enjoy your relationship with your best friend without sharing or acting on your feelings of sexual attraction.

7 | SEXUAL FULFILLMENT
IN ELDER YEARS

W HO WOULD HAVE GUESSED? When most of us were sixteen, we thought that "older folks" stopped having sex when they were sixty—and maybe even sooner. If our grandparents were living, they may have shared a bed, but we couldn't imagine that they did anything more than sleep in it.

Now some of us are grandparents. As we move into our fifties, sixties, seventies, and even eighties, we're amazed that we could have been so naive when we were sixteen! Comprehensive studies now affirm that more than two-thirds of older men and more than half of older women assert that a sexual relationship is important to them. One-fourth of men older than seventy-five say they have sex at least once a week. Even if one allows for a brag factor, the number is still significant.

We all dread those oncoming wrinkles. The face-lift business is growing by leaps and bounds. Yet don't we all know that lovely old couple, proud of the crow's feet that belie their advanced years, who still have that certain gleam in their eye for each other? They still hum that Cole Porter tune familiar to them more than a half century ago: "That's why I ask the Lord above, 'What is this thing called love?'" They still haven't figured out the mystery of love. After all these years they still can't explain it. They only know there is no one else in the world for them.

ONE BIG HAPPY: *By Rick Detorie*

Copyright © 2000 Rick Detorie and Creators Syndicate. Reprinted by permission.

Every new study affirms that part of the mystery is that they still find joy in sex. In fact, many women report that their husbands are more romantic at seventy than they were at thirty. No wonder the audience reacted with loud applause when Jay Leno asked Jimmy Carter about his sex life and the bashful former president, well into his seventies, replied, "Better than ever!"

Yes, sexual desires and habits change over the years. No, they don't go away. In fact, a lifetime of a good relationship in marriage often means that sex is even more meaningful and, yes, even more pleasurable, when we become elders.

Even the Bible seems to affirm our desire for sexual pleasure in old age. When Abraham and Sarah are promised a son in their old age, Sarah's response is, "After I have grown old, and my husband is old, shall I have pleasure?" At his alleged advance age, Abraham might have been acquainted with what we now call ED—erectile dysfunction. For Sarah, is becoming pregnant only a matter of conception? Maybe so. But is it possible that she also welcomes the possibility of finding pleasure again?

Then there's that fascinating text in the first chapter of 1 Kings. By now King David is old—and cold! How do you keep an old king warm? His servants tell the king they will search for a woman and "let her lie in your bosom, so that my lord the king may be warm." And "so they searched for a beautiful girl throughout all the territory of Israel" until they found Abishag. Now isn't it fair to ask, "Why a beautiful young woman"? If warmth was the only issue, why wouldn't they have looked for any woman? Did they think someone beautiful was needed to warm the king's heart and body? The text makes it clear that Abishag was a virgin and that David did not (could not?) have genital sex with her. But we are left with some interesting questions: Though there was snow on the roof, were the fires still burning in the furnace? And would this help to keep the old king warm?

IT STARTS BEFORE YOU GET OLD

In this chapter we describe in some detail how an elderly couple can keep their sexual response alive. First, however, we need to accent again the theme that runs through this book from beginning to end, namely that sex is a whole lot more than physical gratification. This is especially important to keep in mind when we speak about the advancing years of life. If a full relationship has not been nurtured over the years, it may well be that physical desire will decline to the point where a couple has little or no inclination for sexual intercourse or other forms of physical gratification. We can't underscore enough the importance of a couple building a complete relationship through years of experience together, through the highs and lows of marriage, through determination to keep building a sense of oneness.

A good relationship includes nurturing of the spirit. Regular worship, participation in holy communion, sharing one's thoughts about God, praying together—all these may seem to have little or no connection with one's sex life. But if life is whole, if body, mind, and spirit are inseparably linked together, then we would all have to agree that sexual gratification is related to our spiritual well-being.

THERE ARE DIFFERENCES

It is fairly well documented that sexual desire differs for men and women. As a rule of thumb, males tend to have a stronger sex drive when they are young and into middle age. And it is not uncommon for a significant number of men to begin to see a decline in sexual potency in their early fifties. Interest and desire may still be quite strong. But the ability to function may not match desire. Shakespeare witnessed to this experience when in *Henry IV* he wrote, "Is it not strange that desire should so many years outlive performance?" This becomes increasingly the case for many men as they move into their sixties, seventies, and beyond.

For a woman there is often an increase in sexual desire when she has passed her childbearing years. Some researchers even claim that a woman's sexual drive is at its peak when she is in her sixties.

A couple who are one in Christ will be sensitive to their differences and will not be embarrassed to discuss these matters. We have said earlier that a young husband needs to be very patient and sensitive, recognizing that it may take his partner longer to be aroused and come to sexual satisfaction. In the elder years, the wife may need to be the one who initiates sexual activity at times. She will soon realize that her husband welcomes these invitations, just as she did when she was young. And just as his initiatives once aroused in her desires that she was not always aware of, so now her initiatives often do the same for him in the elder years. Many couples have made this discovery and testify that their sex lives at sixty are better, much better in fact, than they were at thirty. At thirty sex may have been more biologically driven, more urgent, more achievement-oriented. Now the accent is more on caring, tenderness, patience, and understanding. Older people have a broader perspective and see more of the whole picture. Now they have a collection of years and years of experiences that become part and parcel of their sex lives.

A LONGER LIFE HAS CHALLENGES

We started this chapter with a reference to our grandparents. Some of us remember a time when it was uncommon to have two grandparents who lived into their sixties or seventies. That changed dramatically in the twentieth century as medical science extended our years. In the early part of the century, strides were made in stopping widespread death from communicable diseases and infections, and there was a dramatic reduction in maternal deaths. More recent successes in the treatment of cancer and heart ailments have been the major contributors to longevity. Whereas once it was common for women to die within months of the discovery of breast cancer, many now experience successful recovery when the disease is detected in its early stages. Similarly, many men who would have once succumbed to prostate cancer now find a complete cure from the disease through surgery or radiation treatment. Folks who would have died in their forties and fifties and sixties in earlier times from heart disease now routinely have angioplasty, heart bypass surgery, or a heart transplant, thus often extending their life span by decades. The average life span in 1900 was fifty years; now we can expect to live to seventy-five or eighty. And those who are now sixty-five can expect to live even longer. Now it's quite normal for a couple to enjoy forty, fifty, even sixty years of married life, and for others to establish a meaningful new marriage following divorce or the death of a spouse. Partners in long-term, same-sex relationships similarly enjoy elder years together. Others, like the widowed or divorced, find renewal in new committed relationships following the death of, or separation from, former partners.

These added years bring with them many pleasures as well as many challenges. Suddenly our whole society is confronted with the issue of how best to meet the needs of the sharply increasing number of the elderly. Now we find ourselves struggling with issues such as scaling down living arrangements, making decisions about nursing-home insurance, helping adult children, coping with decreasing mobility, and many other matters. In spite of remarkable advances, many diseases and other limitations now loom large—Alzheimer's disease, senility, osteoporosis, blindness, joint replacement, strokes, heart ailments—to mention only a few.

In the midst of the good news about living longer, it's important to insert a note of caution. It's an established fact that many older folks do not seek treatment for health problems unless and until the problems become life-threatening. And it's also well known that all too many patients are embarrassed to speak with their medical doctors about sexual issues. Nor are many doctors inclined to inquire about it. Too often, it's a case of "don't ask, don't tell": Doctors don't ask, and patients don't tell. Because such silence prolongs frustration and hinders life fulfillment, we strongly encourage doctors to ask and patients to tell. There is an abundance of hope and healing for people with sexual problems.

Some medications have a direct impact on sexual response. If doctors are reluctant to mention it, patients should ask forthrightly, "Will this medication have any effect on my sex life?" After all, it's your life—your sex life.

ASSUMPTIONS TO BE CHALLENGED

Seldom mentioned as an issue for the elderly is sexuality. It's assumed that it will take care of itself; that the elderly seldom, if ever, think about sex; that desire goes away when a mate dies; that one can turn off sexual desire if a mate becomes incapacitated or loses interest in sex; that by this stage of life there's no need to learn new ways to express love and affection; that a woman loses interest in sex after menopause; that when a man first experiences erectile dysfunction he's on a downhill slope sexually.

Copyright © Tribune Media Services, Inc. All rights reserved.
Reprinted with permission.

All of these assumptions, of course, are wrong. The question is: How can we best deal with our sexual desires and meet our sexual needs in the elder years?

For starters, let it be said that a couple can do anything that is *mutually pleasurable*. The accent is on both words.

It should be *mutual*. A couple should agree together on what they want to do in their sexual life. We've already stated several times that good communication is the key to good sex. Let us say it again: It's all right to talk about sex, openly and frankly. In fact, we might even say that in the elder years it's more important than ever. If one partner desires to express love in a new way, it should be discussed in loving and caring dialogue, rather than buried or explored in a selfish manner by one partner.

It's also important that whatever is done should be for the mutual *pleasure* of both partners. Anything painful or abusive is out-of-bounds. Sex is meant to be enjoyable. Things never tried before may bring no pleasure whatsoever. On the other hand, they may hold surprise and *pleasure* never imagined. As a couple becomes more comfortable and more experienced with new expressions of affection, they will discover that their sex lives are more enjoyable than they ever could have imagined. No wonder many older women who have a healthy sex life say that they experience orgasm more often now than when they were younger.

Sexual practice, of course, will vary from couple to couple. What one set finds delightful and fulfilling may bring disappointment to another. If the latter is the case, there's no need for embarrassment and surely no need to refrain from trying other new avenues of sexual pleasure.

SOME SPECIFIC SUGGESTIONS

As in many other aspects of life, we need to be both caring and creative in our lovemaking. Even after many years, we haven't learned everything about our partners or even about ourselves. In a relationship of love and trust, we can teach and guide one another in ways that provide mutual pleasure, continued sexual satisfaction, and delight. This becomes increasingly important as it becomes more difficult for some people to achieve sexual satisfaction. So let's be candid about ways in which a sexual relationship can be enhanced.

Men get pleasure from fondling and caressing a woman's breasts; a woman gets pleasure from receiving and giving pleasure through her breasts. At times this may be all that is needed to satisfy the sexual impulses of older folks.

Both sexes enjoy it when the genitals are fondled and caressed. When done gently and tenderly it can bring profound delight to both partners. Again, this may be sufficient at times to meet one's need for sexual fulfillment.

We've seen a revolution in sexual response for the elderly with the advent of drugs like Viagra. Such medicines have made it possible for some men—as well as some women—to improve their ability to have sex and to achieve a response that they have not had in years. We should welcome and celebrate these discoveries, even as we give thanks for medications that may help us in other areas of life.

We are careful to say that these medications help "some," since it is now well-established that a significant number of persons either cannot take certain medications because of their side effects or do not get the desired results from a drug. For example, Viagra works for about 70 percent of the men who use it. That means that there are millions who get no help from this revolutionary drug. Severe cases of diabetes, significant damage to nerve cells as a result of surgery or an accident, certain medications, psychological blocks—any number of factors may diminish sexual response.

What are these persons to do if they have a strong desire for sex but cannot function in the usual ways, even with the help of a medication? We would encourage them to explore other avenues. Many men, for example, have been helped by injection therapy. By having a blood-vessel relaxant injected into the penis, they are able to achieve a satisfactory erection. The danger is that sometimes scar tissue can build up from repeated injections. Regular checkups with a specialist are crucial. Others use a vacuum-tube device that enlarges the penis and makes intercourse possible (as noted earlier, a similar device is now available to help women experience orgasm). Still others have a device implanted in the penis that allows them to simulate a natural erection. This process, of course, involves surgery and is irreversible.

Others have found gratification in oral sex. Some are repelled by the very thought of engaging in this form of sexual activity, and we believe their feelings should be respected. But we also believe that any mutually acceptable sexual activity, when done in the right setting and for mutual pleasure is good and appropriate. Many elderly couples find that they achieve greater satisfaction from manual and/or oral stimulation than from conventional intercourse and learn that an erection is not essential for a fully satisfying orgasm for either the man or the woman. While there is no evidence that intercourse is dangerous for people with heart ailments, those with heart trouble or other limiting diseases often discover that they can enjoy sexual fulfillment without the intense physical exertion that often accompanies genital intercourse. Reports also indicate that some women are not happy with their husband's use of drugs like Viagra. Suddenly their sex lives are focused on the husband's penis. They may have learned to appreciate and enjoy sex that is more diffused, more concerned with all of their emotions, rather than centered on the pleasure of orgasm. They discover that without orgasm their lovemaking can still be very pleasurable and life-giving.

Older adults can also learn something from those who are physically handicapped. When a partner is suddenly left without the capacity to have sex in the usual manner, does all sexual activity stop for a couple? Of course not. They find new ways to experience sexual fulfillment by learning from books, seeking the help of therapists, and joining groups that help them understand their challenges.

Though they may not like to think of themselves in this way, or may be too proud to admit it, many elders are in fact sexually handicapped. That is no reason, however, to refrain from exploring new ways to enjoy sex. The adventuresome will find pleasures they assumed were only for their youth. They even may discover greater sexual delight than they have ever known.

Since this book is not intended to be a definitive sex manual, we would encourage those who want to explore new ways to find sexual pleasure to go to a bookstore or public library and look for books that deal with this subject. They are usually found in the sections designated "psychology" or "human behavior." You will find that they run the full gamut of sexual activity, including some that will shock and surprise you. You need to read these books as you would read a menu in a restaurant. You know you won't like certain things and therefore don't order them. Maybe you've already tried them. On the other hand, you may find something you've never even thought of or known about before. In loving and mutual exchange, you and your mate may decide to try something new. There's no harm in reading about these things, discussing them as a couple, and then deciding which, if any, you feel comfortable exploring together.

KEEPING HEALTHY— ONE KEY TO GOOD SEX

This may be an appropriate place to put in a good word about the importance of overall fitness and its connection to a good sex life. Maintaining a good diet, which includes reducing fatty foods and increasing the intake of vegetables, fruits, and high-fiber grains, will not only enhance your general health; it will improve your sex life as well.

Some are able to maintain a regimen of vigorous exercise well into their elder years. Sooner or later, however, most of us will be handicapped by some kind of illness or limitation. The worst thing we can do is turn in on ourselves, pity ourselves, and give up our zest for life. Even with limitations most everyone can be involved in some ways to maintain fitness and vigor. Short walks, floor exercises, stationary cycles—do anything you can to keep your body toned. The benefits will spill over into your sex life.

WHEN YOU ARE ALONE OR ABANDONED SEXUALLY

Now comes the difficult question: What about sex when you are left alone by death or divorce? Or when your partner is still living but unable or unwilling to have sex? What if your partner, although able to do so, refuses to explore new ways to give and receive sexual pleasure? What happens when your partner moves into the dark world of Alzheimer's disease or early senility?

Those who are alone may convince themselves that sex is no longer important, but there is a difference between saying one is no longer interested, on the one hand, and having no opportunity for a sexual relationship, on the other. For these persons it is wise to remember that sex is more than what happens in bed. It is part of a total relationship, a full life. Enjoying hugs in an appropriate way, cultivating friendships, fantasizing, self-pleasuring—these and more can keep alive one's identity as a sexual person.

What about those who have lost interest in sex but whose mate continues to have a strong desire for it? We would urge you to explore carefully and thoroughly the reasons this may be the case. Begin with a good physical exam. Review your medications with your doctor to determine if any may have side effects that suppress sexual desire and ability. There may be physiological reasons that you have lost interest. There may be surgical procedures or medications that will restore some or all of your interest in sex. You owe it to both your mate and yourself to seek to reawaken this important part of your relationship.

If there is no physical basis for a lack of interest, one should explore whether there may be psychological reasons for it. Guilt carried all the way from childhood and youth, shame from abuse or rape, a troubled conscience over an affair, the absence of a sexually stimulating partner—these are only a few of the reasons one might have difficulty getting interested in sex. Whatever the cause, one should seek the help of a good, reputable therapist. Why go on and on depriving yourself of the joys and pleasures of sex in the elder years when all of your life could be enhanced and enriched by healthful sexual activity? You owe it to your partner to deal with these issues and, in so doing, to fulfill promises made at marriage to give yourself without reservation to your mate as a "one flesh" partner.

But what about those older couples who have come to the mutual understanding that sex is not a necessary or even desirable part of their lives? They have been companions for years and years. They gradually stopped having genital sex, but it had no effect on their relationship. They enjoy living as good mates and good friends. We affirm them. There's nothing that says that every couple must have sex so that their marriage will be kept alive. Some have come to the happy conclusion that there are all kinds of things they would rather do together than engage in sex.

There are many, however, who would like to enjoy some form of sexual activity but have resigned themselves to grin and bear it, and forgo sex. They sublimate their sexual desires. They get busy with other kinds of activities that will take their minds away from what they have lost. They think that if they keep active enough and get physically tired enough, thoughts about sex will go away. And they may. Or they may not.

Others use a mate's incapacity or unwillingness to have sex as an excuse to develop another relationship. "My husband has Alzheimer's disease. He's like a dead man to me. This could go on for years. Why is it wrong for me to go to bed on occasion with that nice, caring widower who lives in our complex?" "If my wife refuses to have sex anymore, why can't I have sex with my female friend whose husband can't function anymore? This is just between us. They'll never need to know and be hurt." "My wife says she doesn't love me anymore. But for the sake of our kids and all the legal and financial complications, we don't want to get a divorce. Why is it a sin for me to sleep with a woman who says she loves me?"

We think there's a better alternative for those elders who have strong sexual desires but who believe, as we do, that the alternatives above are usually wrong. It's the same advice we give to teenagers—find release and fulfillment in self-pleasuring. The dynamics are much the same for elders as they are for teens. Self-pleasuring, in and of itself, is not wrong. Like anything else in life, it can become self-defeating and destructive. But when self-pleasuring is done for both release and fulfillment, it can keep one from being preoccupied with sex and from the frustration that often accompanies the denial of sexual urges.

What is missing in self-pleasuring is, of course, the real and not just imagined, affection and touch of a loving companion. This is certainly a significant absence, but we believe that such sharing is appropriate and ultimately fulfilling only in equivalent of marriage relationships. It is wiser and, in the long term, more fulfilling to those who are not in such a relationship to find sexual satisfaction in self-pleasuring and to find the fulfillment of affection and friendship in nongenital relationships.

IT'S IN THE BIBLE

We realize that our specific suggestions for sexual fulfillment in the elder years may raise some eyebrows and even cause some to wonder if we've lost our sanity. For that reason let us reflect again on the biblical roots of human sexuality, this time from that seldom-read book in the Old Testament—the Song of Songs. Tucked away between Psalms and the major prophets, it's easily overlooked. We believe, however, that it is crucial to our understanding of how believers ought to view sex and sexual activity. And for those in the elder years who want to continue to find joy and fulfillment in sex, we can think of no better biblical source.

Song of Songs is really an ancient love song, typical, in many ways, of what can be found in the literature of other ancient civilizations in the Orient. What distinguishes the Song of Songs from these others, however, is that it celebrates erotic sexual love without deifying it, on the one hand, or making it pornographic, on the other.

This book of the Bible is so candid and forthright about erotic love that it has often been allegorized as an expression of God's love for Israel or, in Christian history, as an example of the love of Christ for his bride, the church. There is nothing wrong with using the text for these purposes. The Bible and life itself are full of illustrations of God's love for the world and for the human family.

But most biblical scholars agree that this was not its original purpose. It was written, they insist, to show that God puts a strong stamp of approval on those legitimate urges that lead two people to desire each other and to love each other with an intensity that can be described only as being "as strong as death" (8:6). Song of Songs is not a treatise on the philosophy of love. It is an earthy description of passionate expressions of physical and emotional love between real people, and all of it is rooted in our nature as beings created by God.

So much sexual talk and writing is centered on genital activity. The Song of Songs does not overlook that important part of lovemaking, but puts it into the full context of a deep relationship. The man admires every part of the one he loves—her eyes, hair, teeth, lips, mouth, cheeks, neck, breasts (1:10; 4:1-5). He looks at her from toe to head, admiring feet, thighs, navel, belly, breasts, neck, eyes, nose, head, hair (7:1-5). She, in turn, loves to cradle his head like "a bag of myrrh that lies between my breasts" (1:13). Her whole being longs for his tender hand to explore the sensitive parts of her body (5:4). He calls her "stately as a palm tree" and says her "breasts are like clusters of the vine" (7:7-8) that he longs to grasp hold of. Just to be near her evokes a strong response: "The scent of your breath (is like) apples" (7:8); the "scent of your garments is like the scent of Lebanon" (4:11).

This erotic ardor is saved from superficial physical activity by the theme that runs from beginning to end of the Song of Songs and that has been our accent in this book. This kind of love is for two who are committed to each other for life. "Many waters cannot quench love, neither can floods drown it" (8:7).

A TIME TO EXPLORE

The Song of Songs is surely full of good and appropriate advice for lovers at any stage of life. But we think it is especially helpful for those in the elder years. At a time when one might be tempted to think that erotic love is for the young, that the best is over and gone, that there are no longer any options for finding pleasure in sex, we need to be encouraged to be more adventuresome than ever. For many folks this is a wonderful time of life. As we wind up our busy years of work and raising a family, we can take time to know each other in new ways. If we are willing to accept it, we now have freedom to relax and have fun in many areas of life, including sexual activity. Spending leisurely mornings together in bed without the need to rush off to work, taking time for naps, reading wholesome love stories together, seeing a good movie, deciding to go to bed earlier than usual—there's no limit to the ways we can foster a relationship and nurture sexual love, even in the elder years of life.

So we end as we began—sex is God's gift for our good. Our sexuality and our spirituality go together. Sex is intended to be life-giving. At times it is the gift that brings a child to a family. At all times it is for re-creation, including finding pleasure and joy in one of God's choicest gifts for all who are created in God's image.

May God bless you with God's good gift of life-giving sex.

QUESTIONS & ANSWERS

Q: My husband and I have been married for nearly forty years and have had a good marriage. But recently my husband has had a problem he won't talk about. A year ago we had a romantic anniversary dinner and afterward were both in the mood, but when the time came he was unable to have sexual relations. I didn't make an issue of it, but it had a big impact on him. The only time he makes sexual overtures now is after he has had too much to drink, and things haven't gone well. If I take the initiative, he seems threatened and withdraws. The worst part is not the absence of sexual relations (I can live with that) but the coldness in our marriage. My husband is silent and sullen, and I don't like living like this. I am sure he doesn't like it either, but I don't know what to do about it. If you can help, I will be grateful.

A: To us, the saddest part of your story is that you and your husband are unable to talk about something that is obviously bothering both of you. His problem is not unusual. Both of you can be grateful that you never experienced it sooner! In fact, he may not have a sexual problem. If he does, he should eventually discuss it with a medical doctor and learn about all the help that is available. But we'd like to suggest a different approach for you to try first. The alcohol at the anniversary dinner and preceding his subsequent attempts to have sexual relations may be the real culprit. Although it sometimes increases desire, alcohol can dramatically decrease male sexual capacity. Fear and anxiety are other culprits. When a man fears that he might not have an erection, and tries hard to make it happen, his anxieties and efforts crowd the very stimulation that alone can create it.

We also remind you and your husband that you can have a great time sexually without having intercourse. In fact, many therapists suggest that couples in your situation make some alcohol-free dates for sexual playfulness with the understanding that whatever happens you will not have intercourse. Some even tell the husband that no matter what his wife does he should not become sexually aroused. What happens then is often delightfully amazing.

We encourage you to share our answer with your husband and to kindly encourage him to join you in some times of loving, sexual playfulness. When you do that, his problem will either disappear or be of far less importance to your mutual sexual fulfillment.

Q: I'm seventy-three and very healthy in every way. More than ten years ago my wife first began to develop symptoms of Alzheimer's disease. By the fifth year she didn't know me any more. I visit her almost every day, but she seems to have no idea who I am. It's as though she's died. In the meantime, I try to live a normal life. I have good friends, both male and female. Among them are some widows and single older women who are attractive to me.

Recently I heard about a man whose wife is like mine. With the approval of his children he had his pastor perform a blessing of some kind so that he and a widow, whose husband had died of Alzheimer's and whose children also affirmed their relationship, could live together as husband and wife. I've resisted any move in that direction, believing that the promise I made to my wife at the altar to be faithful until death parts us needs to be honored. What do you think?

A: We think you've chosen the right course and that you should continue to live according to your conscience. We believe, as you do, that promises made before God for lifelong fidelity should be kept.

At the same time, we do not want to judge the man you mention. The key is that the man and his female friend did not act in isolation from those who are important to them. They sought and secured the blessing of their children and their pastor. All of them apparently believed that his wife had in fact "died" as far as their marriage was concerned, and that they were now free to enter a new relationship with God's blessing.

In agonizing situations such as this, each of us must act in accordance with our understanding of God's will for us. We affirm your decision not to become involved in an intimate sexual relationship and encourage you to keep up the strong social contacts you have with both male and female friends. If you find occasional sexual gratification through self-pleasuring, we don't think it's wrong. You also may find it helpful to discuss your feelings with an understanding counselor or with your pastor. Through it all, be assured of God's compassionate care for you and your wife.

Q: My wife and I have been married for thirty-five years and are both retired. We have had a good marriage and have a great family, but she has never been interested in sex, and now our sexual relationship has diminished to almost nothing. In fact she has told me, in effect, that she'd be just as happy if we'd forget about sex altogether.

We have recently moved into a large apartment complex that has an exercise room and swimming pool. I am into physical fitness and spend a lot of time working out and swimming. While doing so I have become acquainted with an attractive woman, and we have spent a lot of time visiting in the hot tub and workout room. She is a little younger than I am and has been divorced for several years. Last week she invited me to stop by her apartment for a drink after we had been working out. She told me that she enjoyed visiting with me. We both behaved ourselves, but some of her moves seemed to be a bit seductive, and I have a hunch that it wouldn't be difficult to get sexually involved.

I have always been faithful to my wife, and my conscience tells me to resist this temptation. But then I wonder, "What harm would it do? I wouldn't be depriving my wife of anything." She spends most of her time watching TV and baby-sitting for our grandchildren who live nearby. She would never need to know about it. And as the saying goes, "What you don't know can't hurt you."

On the other hand, it would certainly add some zest and satisfaction to my life and might even make me a better husband. I would probably be more cheerful and easier to live with. I don't want a divorce, but I would like to live a little before I die. What do you think I should do?

A: We think you are wise to be wary and that you should listen to your conscience. Let your life be ruled by your brains and not your hormones.

Getting involved in such an affair would not make you a better husband. It would make you a deceiver and a cheat and could wreck your marriage and bring much pain to yourself and your family. Even if your wife never learned about it, you would know that you were living a lie and would be constantly fearful that the truth would come out. You would learn in your own experience that adultery isn't just against a commandment in the Bible; it is against the people we love!

Therefore, we encourage you to cool it with this woman and do something to bring some new life into your marriage. Have you honestly and kindly shared how you feel about your lack of sexual fulfillment? Has she shared her feelings with you? If you can't communicate that way, we encourage you to see a competent marriage counselor. Several studies have indicated that women your wife's age are more sexually responsive than they were in their twenties. Perhaps there are specific problems in your relationship that can be corrected. You will never know unless you check it out. Both you and your wife might be delightfully surprised by what can happen in your sexual relationship.

In the meantime, if your wife rebuffs your sexual initiatives, we encourage you to resolve your sexual frustrations through self-pleasuring, which is certainly safer and probably, in the long run, no less satisfying than getting involved in an affair.

When tempted to do something questionable, we should ask ourselves: (1) "Is this something I'd like my family and most respected friends to know about?" and (2) "Is this something I will likely be grateful for five, ten, twenty years from now?" If the answer to those questions is no, we'd best not do it!

CONCLUSION

HAD WE EXPECTED TO PLEASE EVERY READER, the first word of this book would never have been written. We've learned from years of experience that few subjects are as divisive as sex. Because we're all sexual beings who bring with us a lifetime of our own individual experience, each of us has an opinion in almost every area of this complex subject.

For this reason, we know that some readers are disappointed that we have not been more assertive in some areas. Why not face reality and affirm genital sex in some situations prior to marriage? Why not approve of sex outside of marriage in cases where a spouse is unwilling or unable to fill that role? Why not put more pressure on churches to ordain persons in same-sex relationships? These are only a small sampling of questions that might be raised from this corner.

In another corner are those readers who are shocked by some of our suggestions. How could we even dare to mention how far some couples might go in sexual exploration prior to marriage? How could we encourage self-pleasuring under any circumstances and accept "moral and emotional equivalent to marriage" relationships? How could we affirm the blessing of committed same-sex unions? How could we explore possibilities for the ordination of qualified persons in such relationships?

Whatever your reaction to this book may be, we hope that you will not miss our major accent—that sex is a wonderful gift from God, given to us for our enjoyment.

The way the Christian church has dealt with sex over the years has often not been helpful. That should come as no surprise to us.

It took most of twenty centuries for many Christians to agree that all people are created equal by God. And we are still on the way. It took most of twenty centuries to give many women their rightful place in our churches and in society. And we are still on the way. It took most of twenty centuries for many of us to see how we have spoiled the gift of creation. And we are still on the way.

Yes, sex, like every other area of life, is darkened by sin. But has the church accented the negative side of sex so much that the positive side has become all but lost? By our faulty understanding have we encouraged a view of sex that is narrow and focused almost entirely on its physical aspects? We can't blame the Bible. Rather, we must blame our faulty interpretation of the Bible, often influenced by the culture around us. The view of the ancient Hebrews was that the gift of sex was to be celebrated and enjoyed. In the early Christian era the idea was promulgated that spirit is good and body is evil. This false perception continues to skew our appreciation not only for sex, but for all the good gifts of creation.

We cannot blame Jesus. Is it a mere coincidence that the first miracle is the blessing of a marriage and all that this relationship brings with it? We cannot blame Paul. He expected the world to end within a short time. All of the energies of the church were to be used to prepare for that event. No wonder he advised against marriage. He was also a first-century man whose view of women often left something to be desired. Yet we forget that even in that setting, he affirmed the goodness of satisfying the sexual needs of one's partner (1 Cor. 7:3). The analogy of marriage, that it is like the relationship of Christ to the church, surely affirms the intimacy of a man and a woman (Eph. 5:25-33).

When Luther broke the pattern of celibacy for priests and nuns, he sometimes spoke in a very narrow way, underscoring the importance of marriage as a way to satisfy rampant and uncontrollable sexual urges. But we sometimes forget the other things he had to say about the goodness of sex as a gift from God to be enjoyed. In his commentary on Genesis 4:1, he reflects on the phrase "Adam knew his wife." This is more than intercourse, writes Luther. "There is no disgrace in what Moses is saying here about God's creation and his blessing. . . ." This, he goes on to say, is a work of the Holy Spirit who "has no misgivings about referring to the copulation or sexual union of husband and wife. This union of man and woman is more than a physical relationship." In their expression of love for each other, notes Luther, there is "feeling and experience. Adam knew Eve, his wife—not objectively or speculatively, but he actually experienced Eve as a woman." What a remarkable and refreshing view of sex! While Luther is speaking specifically of marriage, his appreciation for the gift of sex as a joyful discovery of oneself as well as a deep encounter with another person can be applied to every phase of life, from childhood to old age. In its proper context, sex is a gift from God for every person. We hope this broader and deeper understanding of sex will be our gift to each reader.

QUESTIONS FOR REFLECTION AND DISCUSSION

To encourage careful consideration of issues raised in these pages, we have prepared the following questions for personal reflection and group discussion. If you decide to use them in a congregational setting, we suggest a five-session series, but depending upon the interest of the people participating it could be either longer or shorter. We recommend a minimum of two sessions, with the first focusing on the basic themes expressed in chapters 1 and 2, and the other one, two, three, or more sessions on issues that are of the most interest and importance to the participants. Instead of necessarily taking the questions in order, group leaders and participants should select which ones they wish to discuss and, of course, may add others as well.

SESSION ONE

Concerning issues raised in the Introduction and chapters 1 and 2, "Life-Giving Sex" and "Life-Degrading Sex":

1. How do you understand the word *sex*? To what does it refer? Do you agree with the understanding presented in the introduction? Why? Why not?

2. Why should Christians be concerned about the total, including sexual, life fulfillment of human beings? How does your understanding of sex relate to issues of "truth and justice"?

3. What understanding of sex did you receive from your parents? From your church?

4. Do you agree that sex is God's gift for our good? Why? Why not?

5. What do you think sex is good for? Discuss the various purposes of sex described in chapter 1. With which do you agree? Disagree?

6. What is sin? What makes it sinful?

7. When is sex sinful? Why?

8. How should we deal with the diversity of biblical examples and teaching concerning sexual morality?

9. Do you agree with the authors' distinction between life-giving and life-degrading sex? Why? Why not? How can this distinction help guide our sexual behavior?

10. Do you agree with the responses given to the concerns raised in the Questions & Answers section at the end of chapter 2? Why? Why not?

SESSION TWO

Concerning issues raised in chapter 3, "Sexual Fulfillment in Marriage":

1. How do you think marriage has changed over the years? Have these changes been for the better? For the worse? Why?

2. How significant is sexual fulfillment to joyful, life-giving marriage? Why?

3. How important is commitment to marital and sexual fulfillment? Why?

4. Do you agree that the brain is the body's most important sex organ? Why? Why not?

5. Discuss the relationship between grace and sexual fulfillment. Do you agree that it is better for a couple to "play at" and not just "work at" their sexual relationship? Why? Why not?

6. Do you agree that there is greater sexual fulfillment when we focus "more on the pleasure we can provide than on the pleasure we can take"? Why? Why not?

7. How do we best cope with what the authors call the "rhythms" of marriage and of sexual experience—sometimes feeling affectionate, sometimes angry, and so on?

8. It is important in marriage to remember that our attitudes, words, and deeds can have unintended consequences. How is this true sexually?

9. Do you agree with Abraham Lincoln that a good guide for decision making is to imagine how we will feel about the decision five to ten years from now? How does this apply sexually?

10. Do you think husbands and wives should tell each other about premarital sexual relationships? Why? Why not?

11. Why is forgiveness essential for a marriage relationship? What should we do when we feel unable to forgive?

12. Discuss the four qualities of (a) mutual love, (b) mutual respect, (c) mutual openness, and (d) mutual faithfulness that are presented as essential to a life-giving sexual relationship. Do you agree that they add up to mutual commitment? Which are most important? Why? What other qualities would you list?

13. If you are married, how important was pre-marriage counseling for you? How could it have been improved? Should the church require it of all couples seeking marriage?

14. Do you think it is all right for a Christian couple to view sexually explicit material together? Is it possible for a film to be

sexually explicit and educational without being pornographic? Why? Why not?

15. When, if ever, it is right for Christians to divorce and remarry? Should the church require that couples being married promise that they will not divorce without having at least six months of marriage counseling? Why? Why not? What do you think they should promise to do?

16. What is wrong with extramarital sexual relationships? Are they ever right? If yes, under what circumstances? Why?

17. What should we do when tempted toward an extramarital affair?

18. For spouses' conversation with each other: Review chapter 3, especially the Questions & Answers section, and then discuss any personal concerns that were brought to mind.

SESSION THREE

Concerning issues raised in chapters 4 and 5, "Sexual Fulfillment When Single" and "Sexual Fulfillment While Living Together":

1. Do you think it is proper for Christians to discuss sexual fulfillment for single persons? Why? Why not?

2. What are the best ways to "enjoy being single"?

3. Discuss what the church can do to help singles "walk in faith." What is your congregation doing? What more could be done?

4. Discuss "self-pleasuring." Do you think that term is better than "masturbation"? Why? Why not? Can self-pleasuring be "God's gift to the celibate"? To those in committed relationships? When is it right? When is it wrong?

5. Are sexual fantasies always sinful? Why? Why not?

6. Do you agree with the authors' warning to those who are divorced or widowed? Why? Why not?

7. Do you agree that couples should wait until they are married before they engage in sexual intercourse? Why? Why not?

8. How long should a couple be engaged? When is engagement too short? Too long?

9. What should a young woman say to a young man who pressures her to prove her love by having sexual relations?

10. What should a young man say to a young woman who makes herself easily available for sexual intercourse?

11. Do you agree that a relationship focused on sex alone will soon "wither and die"? Why? Why not?

12. Discuss Dr. Eleanor Hamilton's alternatives to intercourse. Do you agree? Why? Why not?

13. Do you agree with the authors' advice "to those who insist on intercourse" (see pp. 77–79)? Why? Why not?

14. Do you agree that wrongful sexual activity is "not only sinful; it is stupid"? Why? Why not?

15. Discuss the common practice of unmarried couples living together. Is this ever right? Why? Why not? What is your opinion of the social-science evidence cited in this chapter?

16. Do you believe there is such a thing as "the moral and emotional equivalent of marriage"? If yes, in what does it consist? Is it possible for a couple to be married in the sight of God but not legally married?

SESSION FOUR

Concerning issues raised in chapter 6, "Sexual Fulfillment in Same-Sex Relationships":

1. How do you understand homosexuality? How have you come to this understanding?

2. Do you agree that our sexual orientation is discovered, not chosen? Why? Why not?

3. Do you think it is possible to change our sexual orientation? Why? Why not? If yes, how?

4. Do you agree that the standards for sexual behavior for homosexuals should be the same as for heterosexuals? Why? Why not? If this is true, what does it imply?

5. Do you believe that there should be laws guaranteeing the human and civil rights of homosexuals, or do you believe that such laws give special rights to homosexuals? Defend your answer.

6. Should the state expand the definition of marriage to include same-sex couples or allow for domestic partnerships or "civil unions" with legal provisions equivalent to marriage? Why? Why not?

7. Should pastors perform "blessing of relationship" services for same-sex couples? Why? Why not? If yes, of what kind? Who should be involved in this decision? What do you think about the suggestion that laypeople conduct such services?

8. Should the church ordain persons in committed, same-sex relationships who are otherwise qualified for pastoral ministry? Why? Why not? If policies prohibiting such ordinations are not changed, should congregations have freedom to ordain such people without being expelled from the church? Why? Why not?

9. Some interpreters believe that the Bible condemns all same-sex activity. Others believe that it condemns only lustful, exploitative

same-sex activity. Still others believe that the Bible says nothing concerning homosexuality as we understand it today. What do you believe? On what do you base this belief?

10. Do you agree that "the New Testament is silent on the question . . . [of] long-term commitments of love and trust between consenting persons of the same gender"? Why? Why not?

11. The authors confess that their views concerning homosexuality have been changed by the testimony of gay and lesbian Christians. Have you heard such Christian witness? If yes, what influence did it have on you? If no, how might you arrange to hear it?

12. Select and discuss some of the specific concerns raised in the Questions & Answers section at the end of this chapter. Do you agree with the authors' responses? Why? Why not?

13. Read the account of one family's pilgrimage of understanding titled "One Family's Story" by Paul Egertson in *Homosexuality and Christian Faith*, ed. Walter Wink (Minneapolis: Fortress Press, 1999). I can be found online at *www.augsburgfortress.org/store/ idetail.asp?ISBN=0806640472*. Once there, scroll down to the "Additional Information" section and click on the "Relatated Essay I" link. Would your discovery of a gay or lesbian relative be similar or different from that described? How would you react?

14. Ponder the account of "Learning About Sex From Sacks" (follow Web directions above and click on "Related Essay II" link). Is it possible that homosexual orientation like Mr. I's vision may be "a strange gift" to be "received with thanksgiving"? Why? Why not?

SESSION FIVE

Concerning issues raised in chapter 7, "Sexual Fulfillment in Elder Years":

1. At what age do you think people lose interest in sex? On what do you base your opinion?

2. At what age do you think people lose their ability for sex? On what do you base this opinion?

3. In what ways do you think that sex is "a whole lot more than physical gratification"?

4. Discuss sexual differences between men and women. Does it surprise you that "some researchers even claim that a woman's sexual drive is at its peak when she is in her sixties"? What do you make of that?

5. If it is true that doctors "don't ask" and patients "don't tell," do you think doctors should start asking and that patients should be frank and honest in telling? Why? Why not?

6. Do you think older couples should try "new avenues of sexual pleasure"? Including genital touching and oral sex? Why? Why not? What limits should be observed?

7. How should older people cope with sexual difficulties that may accompany certain illnesses or follow surgery? Do you agree that intercourse is not necessary for sexual fulfillment? Why? Why not?

8. Do you agree that couples should read books that deal with elder sex fulfillment? Why? Why not?

9. Do you agree that fantasizing and self-pleasuring are appropriate means of life-giving sexual fulfillment for elder persons? Why? Why not?

10. Is there anything wrong with older couples who "enjoy living as good mates and good friends" without genital sex? Why? Why not?

11. Reflect on the situations in the Questions & Answers section at the end of this chapter. Do you agree with the authors' responses? Why? Why not?

12. How have your opinions been affirmed, challenged, or changed by reading this book and participating in these discussions? Has the reading, reflecting, and discussing been helpful or hurtful? Why?

WORKS CITED

Bonhoeffer, Dietrich. *Letters and Papers from Prison*, revised edition. Originally published as *Prisoners for God*, ed. Eberhard Bethge (New York: Macmillan, 1967), 49.

Chambers, Oswald. *My Utmost for His Highest* (New York: Dodd, Mead, 1965 [1935]), 73, 119.

The Diagnostic and Statistical Manual of Mental Disorders, Fourth Edition (*DSM*-IV) (Washington, D.C.: American Psychiatric Association, 1994), 505.

Frost, Gerhard. "Loose-Leaf," *Seasons of a Lifetime: A Treasury of Meditations* (Minneapolis: Augsburg, 1989), 57.

Geisel, Theodor (Dr. Seuss). *Green Eggs and Ham* (New York: Beginner Books; distributed by Random House, 1960), 62.

Gudorf, Christine E. *Body, Sex, and Pleasure: Reconstructing Christian Sexual Ethics* (Cleveland: Pilgrim Press, 1995), 106.

Hamilton, Eleanor. *Sex, with Love: A Guide for Young People* (Boston: Beacon Press, 1978), 38, 39.

Jacobowitz, Ruth S. *150 Most-Asked Questions about Midlife Sex, Love and Intimacy* (New York: William Morrow and Company, 1996), 137.

Luther, Martin. "Lectures on Genesis," in *Luther's Works*, vol. 1 (St. Louis: Concordia Publishing House, 1958), 238–41.

Masters, William H., and Virginia Johnson. *The Pleasure Bond* (Boston: Little, Brown, 1974), 36.

Morris, Thomas V. *Making Sense of It All: Pascal and the Meaning of Life* (Grand Rapids, Mich.: Eerdmans, 1992), 17.

Popenoe, David, and Barbara Dafoe Whitehead. *Should We Live Together? What Young Adults Should Know About Cohabitation before Marriage* (New Brunswick, N.J.: National Marriage Project, Rutgers University, 1999), 1–3, 14.

———. *The State of Our Unions: The Social Health of Marriage in America* (New Brunswick, N.J.: National Marriage Project, Rutgers University, 1999), 16.

Shaw, George Bernard. "Thoughts on the Business of Life," *Forbes* (November 20, 1995): 242.

Wall, James. *The Christian Century* (July 19–26, 2000): 739.

Whitehead, Alfred North. *The Concept of Nature* (Ann Arbor: University of Michigan Press, 1997 [1920]), 163.

RESOURCES FOR
FURTHER READING
AND REFLECTION

A LL INFORMATION is subject to change. The publisher and the authors do not necessarily endorse these resources but offer them for the reader's personal research and evaluation.

BOOKS

Balch, David L., ed. *Homosexuality, Science, and the "Plain Sense" of Scripture* (Grand Rapids, Mich.: Eerdmans, 2000). Victor Paul Furnish of Perkins School of Theology says that this book "will certainly take its place among the very best of recent volumes devoted to how the church should view homosexuality." Ralph W. Klein of Lutheran School of Theology says that "[these essays] also provide a sterling model of how the church can disagree with itself publicly and responsibly, passionately and respectfully." We especially commend the chapter by David E. Fredrickson of Luther Seminary dealing with Romans 1:24-27 and 1 Corinthians 6:9, 10.

Benne, Robert. *Ordinary Saints: An Introduction to the Christian Life* (Philadelphia: Fortress Press, 1988). See especially chapter 7, "Marriage and Family Life."

Block, Joel D., with Susan Crain Bakos. *Sex over 50* (West Nyack, N.Y.: Parker Publishing, 1999). This technique-oriented book is exceedingly specific and somewhat sensational in presentation. We have reservations concerning parts of it but are sure that some readers will find it helpful.

Boteach, Shmuley. *Kosher Sex: A Recipe for Passion and Intimacy* (New York: Doubleday, 1999). Reflections on sexual fulfillment from a rabbi's perspective.

Cahill, Lisa Sowle. *Between the Sexes: Foundations for a Christian Ethics of Sexuality* (Philadelphia: Fortress Press, 1985). Cahill, a Roman Catholic, is professor of Christian ethics at Boston College, Chestnut Hill, Massachusetts.

Countryman, L. William. *Dirt, Greed, and Sex: Sexual Ethics in the New Testament and Their Implications for Today* (Philadelphia: Fortress Press, 1988). This scholarly study discusses issues of purity and property, as well as sexual morality of the Old and New Testaments.

Erdahl, Lowell O. *Ten for Our Time: A New Look at the Ten Commandments* (Lima, Ohio: C.S.S. Publishing, 1986). See especially chapter 6, "Sacramental Sex," which briefly discusses some of the contentious issues considered more fully in this book.

Erdahl, Lowell O., and Carol J. Erdahl. *Be Good to Each Other: An Open Letter on Marriage* (Minneapolis: Augsburg, 1991). See especially chapter 5, "Alone Together," and chapter 8, "Faithfulness in Equal Marriage."

Francoeur, Robert T., Martha Cornog, and Timothy Perper, eds., *Sex, Love and Marriage in the 21st Century: The Next Sexual Revolution* (San Jose: toExcel, 1999). This volume contains twenty-two stories by women and men who have sought to combine spirituality and sexuality in unconventional relationships. We affirm the book for study and reflection but do not affirm all of the "unorthodox" explorations in quest of sexual fulfillment that the authors describe.

Francoeur, Robert T., general ed., and Patricia Barthalow Koch and David L. Weis, eds. *Sexuality in America: Understanding Our Sexual Values and Behavior* (New York: Continuum, 1998). A basic reference work by forty-six American sexologists that deals with the ethnic, racial, and religious complexity of American sexuality.

Gudorf, Christine E. *Body, Sex, and Pleasure: Reconstructing Christian Sexual Ethics* (Cleveland: Pilgrim Press, 1994). James B. Nelson, former professor of Christian ethics, United Theological Seminary, describes this book as "An enormously important, honest, and clear sexual ethics for our time."

Hamilton, Eleanor. *Sex with Love: A Guide for Young People* (Boston: Beacon Press, 1978). Candid reflections on love and sex for teenagers and young adults.

Harris, Robie H. *It's Perfectly Normal* (Cambridge: Candlewick Press, 1994). This book for teenagers is "about changing bodies, growing up, sex, and sexual health." It contains dozens of explicit color illustrations by Michael Emberley, and discusses just about everything an adolescent would like to know. Concerning it, Ann Landers says, "At last . . . a book for young people about sex and reproduction in language they can understand, plus pictures they will enjoy."

————. *It's So Amazing! A Book About Eggs, Sperm, Birth, Babies and Families* (Cambridge: Candlewick Press, 1999). Similar to *It's Perfectly Normal,* but written for readers ages seven to twelve.

Jacobowitz, Ruth S. *150 Most-Asked Questions About Midlife Sex, Love and Intimacy: What Women and Their Partners Really Want to Know* (New York: Hearst Books, 1995). Frank answers to questions raised by women.

Jersild, Paul. *Spirit Ethics: Scripture and the Moral Life* (Minneapolis: Fortress Press, 2000). Note especially chapter 7 on homosexuality.

Jung, Patricia Beattie, and Ralph F. Smith. *Heterosexism: An Ethical Challenge* (Albany, N.Y.: State University of New York Press, 1993). When they wrote this book, Jung, a Roman Catholic laywoman, and Smith, an ordained Lutheran pastor, were professors at Wartburg Theological Seminary. A scholarly, biblically grounded presentation that challenges us to overcome our heterosexual perspectives and prejudices concerning people of homosexual orientation.

Klein, Marty, and Riki Robbins. *Let Me Count the Ways: Discovering Great Sex without Intercourse* (New York: Jeremy P. Tarcher/Putnam, 1998). Frank encouragement concerning "outercourse" avenues to sexual fulfillment.

Masters, William H., and Virginia E. Johnson. *The Pleasure Bond: A New Look at Sexuality and Commitment* (Boston: Little, Brown & Co, 1970). Note especially chapter 8, "What Sexual Fidelity Means in a Marriage," and chapter 12, "Commitment: The Pleasure Bond."

McManus, Michael J. *Marriage Savers: Helping Your Friends and Family Stay Married* (Grand Rapids, Mich.: Zondervan Publishing House, 1993). A how-to guide containing practical, biblical advice to strengthen and save marriages.

Nelson, James B. *Embodiment: An Approach to Sexuality in Christian Theology* (Minneapolis: Augsburg Publishing House, 1978). This is a classic in Christian sexual ethics.

———. *Between Two Gardens: Reflections on Sexuality in Religious Experience* (New York: Pilgrim Press, 1983). Continued exploration of concerns raised in *Embodiment*.

Nelson, James B. *Body Theology* (Louisville: Westminster/John Knox, 1992). Nelson says that this book seeks to "take our body experiences seriously as an occasion of revelation." This book specifically deals with "sexual theology, men's issues, and biomedical ethics."

———. *The Intimate Connection: Male Sexuality, Masculine Spirituality* (Philadelphia: Westminster Press, 1988). This book seeks to share "an understanding of the true meaning of love."

Nelson, James B., and Sandra P. Longfellow, eds. *Sexuality and the Sacred: Sources for Theological Reflection Theology* (Louisville: Westminster/John Knox, 1994). This is a collection of thirty-four essays by as many authors who unite in the conviction that sexuality is more than genital sex and that it is intended by God to be a basic dimension of our spirituality.

Nissinen, Martti. *Homoeroticism in the Biblical World: A Historical Perspective* (Minneapolis: Fortress Press, 1998). Note especially the concluding chapter, "Homoeroticism in the Biblical World and Homosexuality Today." This well-documented work emphasizes the fact that no biblical texts specifically address homosexuality as we understand it today.

Olson, David H., and Amy K. Olson. *Empowering Couples: Building on Your Strengths* (Minneapolis: Life Innovations, 2000). A practical guide for couples, based upon more than twenty years of research on couples in the Prepare/Enrich Program created by David H. Olson.

Scroggs, Robin. *The New Testament and Homosexuality* (Philadelphia: Fortress Press, 1983). A pioneering study that challenges traditional interpretations of frequently quoted biblical texts.

Sonnenberg, Roger. *Human Sexuality: A Christian Perspective* (St. Louis, Mo.: Concordia Publishing House, 1998). Explicit discussion of sexual concerns by a Missouri Synod Lutheran pastor.

Spong, John Shelby. *Living in Sin: A Bishop Rethinks Human Sexuality* (San Francisco: Harper and Row, 1988). A provocative discussion of many issues concerning biblical interpretation and sexual ethics.

Timmerman, Joan. *Sexuality and Spiritual Growth* (New York: Crossroad Publishing, 1992). Insightful Roman Catholic presentation concerning sexuality and spirituality.

Wallerstein, Judith, and Sandra Blakeslee. *Second Chances: Men, Women and Children, a Decade after Divorce* (New York: Ticknor and Fields, 1989). This book contains information intended to help persons considering divorce have realistic expectations concerning life following divorce.

BOOKLET

Gilbert, Susan. "What To Do About Erectile Dysfunction," published by Harvard Health Publications, 1999. This special report from Harvard Medical School is available for $16.00 from the publisher: P.O. Box 421073, Palm Coast, FL, 32142–1073. It includes a list of recommended books and organizations.

VIDEO / DISCUSSION MATERIALS

"Called to Witness." A video documentary "about the courageous struggle for gay and lesbian rights within the Lutheran Church." Produced by Pam Walton Productions, P.O. Box 391025, Mountain View, CA, 94039; (650) 960-3414. This fifty-nine-minute videotape with discussion guide is available for $60.00 plus $6.00 shipping and handling.

"Talking Together as Christians about Homosexuality: A Guide for Congregations." Produced by the Division for Church in Society, Evangelical Lutheran Church in America, 1999. This set includes a participation book, leader guide, and ninety-minute video presenting "Two Ethical Perspectives" and is available from the Augsburg Fortress Publishers Distribution Center; call (800) 328-4648 and ask for Code 67-1256, ISBN 6-0001-1117-7. A companion eighty-eight-minute video, "Stories of Gay People and Family Members," again reflecting differing ethical perspectives with presentations by gay and lesbian persons is available from the same source. Ask for Code 67-1257, ISBN 6-0001-1118-5.

ASSOCIATIONS AND ORGANIZATIONS FOCUSING ON HUMAN SEXUALITY AND MARRIAGE

American Association of Marital and Family Therapy (AAMFT), 1133 15th St. N.W., Suite 300, Washington, DC 20005; (202) 452-0109. This group provides information regarding marriage and family counseling.

American Association of Sex Educators, Counselors, and Therapists, P.O. Box 238, Mount Vernon, IA 523114–0238. If you send a self-addressed, stamped envelope, they will provide a list of certified sex therapists in your area.

Association for Couples for Marriage Enrichment (ACME), P.O. Box 10596, Winston Salem, NC 27108; (800) 634-8325. The ACME is a resource for information concerning marriage enrichment programs.

Engaged Encounter, 5 Tara Dr., Pittsburgh, PA 15209; (412) 487-5116. Offers information concerning denominational retreats for engaged couples. Engaged Encounter groups are highly regarded for their enhancement of communications skills.

Interfaith Engaged Encounter, 509 S. Forest St., Denver, CO 80220; (303) 753-9407. Offers information on interfaith retreats for engaged couples.

Life Innovations, Inc., Prepare/Enrich, P.O. Box 190, Minneapolis, MN 55440–0190; (651) 635-0511, (800) 331-1661; *cs@lifeinnovations.com; www.lifeinnovations.com.* The source of the excellent Prepare/Enrich Marriage Preparation and Marriage Enrichment materials.

National Marriage Encounter, 4704 Jamerson Pl., Orlando, FL 32807; (800) 828-3351. Source of information concerning interdenominational weekend retreats.

Retrouvaille, 231 Valentine, Houston, TX 77015; (800) 470-2230. A Catholic, lay-led movement similar to Marriage Encounter for couples in troubled marriages. All faiths are welcome.

Sexuality Information and Education Council of the United States (SIECUS) 130 W. 42nd St., Suite 350, New York, NY 10036–7802; (212) 819-9770. SIECUS is a "national nonprofit organization founded in 1964 to affirm that sexuality is a natural and healthy part of living."

Worldwide Marriage Encounter, 2210 E. Highland Ave., #106, San Bernardino, CA 92404; (800) 795-LOVE; *www.wwme.org.* Source of information concerning denominational weekend retreats.

CHRISTIAN ORGANIZATIONS FOCUSING ON LESBIAN AND GAY CONCERNS

Affirmation/Mormons, P.O. Box 46022, Los Angeles, CA 90046.

Affirmation/United Methodists, P.O. Box 1021, Evanston, IL 60204.

American Baptists Concerned, 872 Erie St., Oakland, CA 94610.

Axios-Eastern and Orthodox Christian Gay Men and Women, 328 W. 17th St., Apt 4F, New York, NY 10011.

Brethren/Mennonite Council for Lesbian and Gay Concerns, P.O. Box 6300, Minneapolis, MN 55406.

Common Bond (former Jehovah's Witnesses and Mormons), P.O. Box 405, Ellwood, PA 16117.

Dignity, Inc. (Roman Catholics), 1500 Massachusetts Ave. N.W., Suite 111, Washington, DC 20025–01894.

Emergence International (Christian Scientists), P.O. Box 9161, San Rafael, CA 94912–9161.

Evangelicals Concerned, 311 E. 72nd St., Suite 1-G, New York, NY 10021.

Friends for Lesbian/Gay Concerns (Quakers), P.O. Box 222, Sumneytown, PA 18084.

Gay, Lesbian, and Affirming Disciples Alliance (Christian Church, Disciples of Christ), P.O. Box 19223, Indianapolis, IN 46219–0223.

Holiness Alliance for Gay/Lesbian Ministries, P.O. Box 60098, Nashville, TN 37206–0098.

Honesty (Southern Baptist Convention), 603 Quail's Run Road, Apt. C-1, Louisville, KY 40207.

Integrity, Inc. (Episcopalians), P.O. Box 19561, Washington, DC 20036–0561.

Lifeline Baptists (All Baptists), 8150 Lakecrest Dr., Greenbelt, MD 20770.

Lutheran Lesbian and Gay Ministries, 152 Church St., San Francisco, CA 94114.

Lutheran Network for Inclusive Vision, P.O. Box 16313, San Diego, CA 92176; (619) 283-0171.

Lutherans Concerned, P.O. Box 10461, Fort Dearborn Station, Chicago, IL 60610–0461.

National Gay Pentecostal Alliance, P.O. Box 1391, Schenectady, NY 12301–1391.

Parents and Friends of Lesbians and Gays, P.O. Box 20308, Denver, CO 80220; *www.pflag.org.*

Presbyterians for Lesbian and Gay Concerns, P.O. Box 38, New Brunswick, NJ 08903–0038.

Reconciling Congregations Program, 3801 N. Keeler Ave., Chicago, IL 60641; (773) 736-5526. This interdenominational Reconciling Congregations Program assists congregations that wish to be open and affirming to gay and lesbian people.

Reformed Church in America Gay Caucus, P.O. Box 8174, Philadelphia, PA 19101–8174.

SDA Kinship International (Seventh-day Adventists), P.O. Box 3840, Los Angeles, CA 90078–3840.

Soul Force, P.O. Box 4467, Laguna Beach, CA 92652. Seeks to apply the principles of Mohandas Gandhi and Martin Luther King Jr. in the struggle for justice for persons of homosexual orientation.

T-E-N (The Evangelical Network), P.O. Box 32441, Phoenix, AZ 85064.

Unitarian Universalists for Lesbian and Gay Concerns, 25 Beacon St., Boston, MA 02108.

United Church Coalition for Lesbian/Gay Concerns (UCC), 18 N. College St., Athens, OH 45701.

Universal Fellowship of Metropolitan Community Churches, 500 Santa Monica Blvd., Suite 304, Los Angeles, CA 90029.

Wingspan Ministry of St. Paul-Reformation Church, 100 N. Oxford St., St. Paul, MN 55104–6540; (651) 224-3371; *www .cyberword.com/spr.* A congregational-based ministry of witness, education, pastoral care, and advocacy on behalf of gay, lesbian, bisexual, and transgender persons and their families and friends.

Note: telephone numbers, e-mail, Web site, and postal addresses are current as of this printing but are subject to change.

ALSO BY THE AUTHORS

Herbert W. Chilstrom: *Hebrews: A New and Better Way; Foundations for the Future; When We Reach for the Sun* (with Jim Klobuchar); *The Many Faces of Pastoral Ministry: Perspectives by Bishops of the Evangelical Lutheran Church in America* (coeditor with Lowell Almen); *Faith and Ferment: An Interdisciplinary Study of Christian Beliefs and Practices* (contributor); *Granlund, the Sculptor and His Work* (contributor); *The Many Faces of Pastoral Ministry: Perspectives by Bishops of the Evangelical Lutheran Church in America* (with Lowell G. Almen); and *Augsburg Sermons* (contributor).

Lowell O. Erdahl: *The Lonely House: Strength for Times of Loss; Be Good to Each Other: An Open Letter on Marriage* (with Carol Erdahl); and *10 Habits of Effective Ministry: A Guide for Life-Giving Pastors.*